TEXAS ★ SINGS

Stories and Verse Celebrating Our State

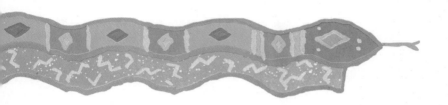

Titles in This Set

Don't Wake the Princess

The World Is Round
Just Like an Orange

We're All in This Together

Y.O.U.

Do You Hear What I See?

The Wolf Is at the Door

Texas Sings

Cover Artist
From a very early age, her family suspected that **Maria Stroster** would become an artist. When she was eight, she formed an apple out of clay she dug from the ground, dried, and painted. To make the apple especially realistic, she bit into it to add teeth marks!

ISBN 0-673-80047-4

Acknowledgments appear on page 160.

2345678910RRS999896959493

TEXAS ★ SINGS

Stories and Verse Celebrating Our State

📖 ScottForesman

A Division of HarperCollins*Publishers*

CONTENTS

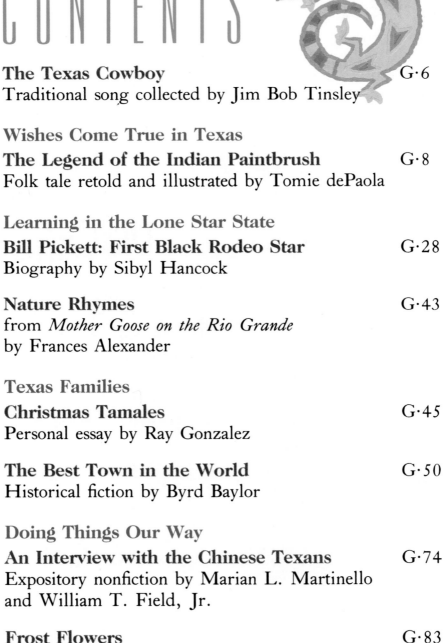

The Texas Cowboy　　　　　　　　　　　G·6
Traditional song collected by Jim Bob Tinsley

Wishes Come True in Texas
The Legend of the Indian Paintbrush　　G·8
Folk tale retold and illustrated by Tomie dePaola

Learning in the Lone Star State
Bill Pickett: First Black Rodeo Star　　G·28
Biography by Sibyl Hancock

Nature Rhymes　　　　　　　　　　　　G·43
from *Mother Goose on the Rio Grande*
by Frances Alexander

Texas Families
Christmas Tamales　　　　　　　　　　G·45
Personal essay by Ray Gonzalez

The Best Town in the World　　　　　　G·50
Historical fiction by Byrd Baylor

Doing Things Our Way
An Interview with the Chinese Texans　G·74
Expository nonfiction by Marian L. Martinello
and William T. Field, Jr.

Frost Flowers　　　　　　　　　　　　G·83
Expository nonfiction by Ilo Hiller

Visiting Huelo y Huela
Personal essay by Marisa Perales

G·89

Land of Big Imaginations
A Writer in Texas
Essay by Joan Lowery Nixon

G·94

You Bet Your Britches, Claude
Humorous fiction by Joan Lowery Nixon

G·100

Hey Little Girl, Miss Mary Mack
from *Apples on a Stick: The Folklore of
Black Children*
Poems collected by Barbara Michels
and Bettye White
Illustrations by Jerry Pinkney

G·116

G·118

Courage, Texas-Style
Elisabet Ney
from *Twenty Texans*
Biography by Betsy Warren

G·120

The Great Red River Raft
Narrative nonfiction by Peter Zachary Cohen

G·128

Deep in the Heart of Texas
Words by June Hershey
Music by Don Swander

G·148

Student Resources
Books to Read
Literary Terms
Glossary

G·150
G·152
G·154

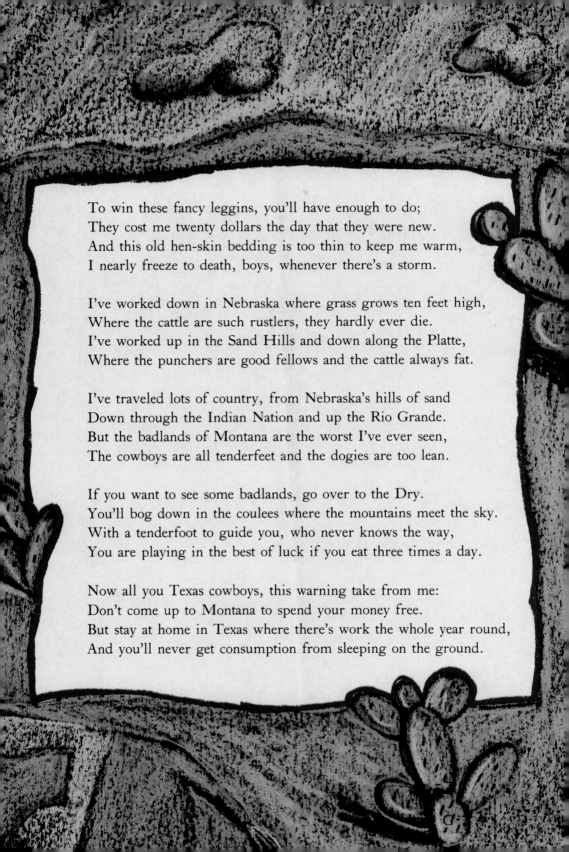

To win these fancy leggins, you'll have enough to do;
They cost me twenty dollars the day that they were new.
And this old hen-skin bedding is too thin to keep me warm,
I nearly freeze to death, boys, whenever there's a storm.

I've worked down in Nebraska where grass grows ten feet high,
Where the cattle are such rustlers, they hardly ever die.
I've worked up in the Sand Hills and down along the Platte,
Where the punchers are good fellows and the cattle always fat.

I've traveled lots of country, from Nebraska's hills of sand
Down through the Indian Nation and up the Rio Grande.
But the badlands of Montana are the worst I've ever seen,
The cowboys are all tenderfeet and the dogies are too lean.

If you want to see some badlands, go over to the Dry.
You'll bog down in the coulees where the mountains meet the sky.
With a tenderfoot to guide you, who never knows the way,
You are playing in the best of luck if you eat three times a day.

Now all you Texas cowboys, this warning take from me:
Don't come up to Montana to spend your money free.
But stay at home in Texas where there's work the whole year round,
And you'll never get consumption from sleeping on the ground.

The Legend of
the Indian Paintbrush

by Tomie dePaola

Many years ago
when the People traveled the Plains
and lived in a circle of teepees,
there was a boy who was smaller
than the rest of the children in the tribe.
No matter how hard he tried,
he couldn't keep up with the other boys
who were always riding, running, shooting their bows,
and wrestling to prove their strength.
Sometimes his mother and father worried for him.

But the boy, who was called Little Gopher,
was not without a gift of his own.
From an early age, he made toy warriors
from scraps of leather and pieces of wood
and he loved to decorate smooth stones
with the red juices from berries
he found in the hills.
The wise shaman of the tribe understood
that Little Gopher had a gift that was special.
"Do not struggle, Little Gopher.
Your path will not be the same as the others.
They will grow up to be warriors.
Your place among the People will be remembered
for a different reason."

And in a few years
when Little Gopher was older,
he went out to the hills alone
to think about becoming a man,
for this was the custom of the tribe.
And it was there that a Dream-Vision came to him.

The sky filled with clouds and out of them
came a young Indian maiden and an old grandfather.
She carried a rolled-up animal skin
and he carried a brush made of fine animal hairs
and pots of paints.

The grandfather spoke.
"My son, these are the tools
by which you shall become great among your People.
You will paint pictures of the deeds of the warriors
and the visions of the shaman,
and the People shall see them and remember them forever."

The maiden unrolled a pure white buckskin
and placed it on the ground.
"Find a buckskin as white as this," she told him.
"Keep it and one day you will paint a picture
that is as pure as the colors
in the evening sky."

And as she finished speaking, the clouds cleared
and a sunset of great beauty filled the sky.
Little Gopher looked at the white buckskin
and on it he saw colors as bright and beautiful
as those made by the setting sun.

Then the sun slowly sank behind the hills,
the sky grew dark,
and the Dream-Vision was over.
Little Gopher returned to the circle of the People.

The next day he began to make soft brushes
from the hairs of different animals
and stiff brushes from the hair of the horses' tails.
He gathered berries and flowers
and rocks of different colors
and crushed them to make his paints.

He collected the skins of animals,
which the warriors brought home from their hunts.
He stretched the skins on wooden frames
and pulled them until they were tight.

And he began to paint pictures . . .

Of great hunts . . .

Of great deeds . . .

Of great Dream-Visions . . .
So that the People would always remember.

But even as he painted,
Little Gopher sometimes longed
to put aside his brushes
and ride out with the warriors.
But always he remembered his Dream-Vision
and he did not go with them.

Many months ago,
he had found his pure white buckskin,
but it remained empty
because he could not find the colors of the sunset.
He used the brightest flowers,
the reddest berries,
        and the deepest purples from the rocks,
            and still his paintings never satisfied him.
            They looked dull and dark.

He began to go to the top of a hill each evening
and look at the colors that filled the sky
to try and understand how to make them.
He longed to share the beauty of his Dream-Vision
with the People.

But he never gave up trying,
and every morning when he awoke
he took out his brushes and his pots of paints
and created the stories of the People
with the tools he had.

One night as he lay awake,
he heard a voice calling to him.
"Because you have been faithful to the People
and true to your gift,
you shall find the colors you are seeking.

"Tomorrow take the white buckskin
and go to the place
where you watch the sun in the evening.
There on the ground you will find what you need."

The next evening as the sun began to go down,
Little Gopher put aside his brushes
and went to the top of the hill
as the colors of the sunset spread across the sky.

And there, on the ground all around him,
were brushes filled with paint,
each one a color of the sunset.
Little Gopher began to paint quickly and surely,
using one brush, then another.

And as the colors in the sky began to fade,
Little Gopher gazed at the white buckskin
and he was happy.
He had found the colors of the sunset.
He carried his painting down
to the circle of the People,
leaving the brushes on the hillside.

And the next day, when the People awoke,
the hill was ablaze with color,
for the brushes had taken root in the earth
and multiplied into plants
of brilliant reds, oranges, and yellows.

And every spring from that time,
the hills and meadows burst into bloom.

And every spring,
the People danced and sang the praises
of Little Gopher who had painted for the People.

And the People no longer called him Little Gopher,
but He-Who-Brought-the-Sunset-to-the-Earth.

Thinking About It

1. You are Little Gopher as a grown man. A young child asks you how the Indian paintbrush got its name. What do you tell the child about yourself and the Indian paintbrush?

2. What are some of the difficulties Little Gopher faces because of his special talent and his task?

3. Little Gopher is a talented painter who shares his talent with others by painting a beautiful sunset. Think of a way you can share one of your talents.

Another Book by Tomie dePaola
In *The Legend of the Bluebonnet,* a young Native American girl knows what she must sacrifice to help her people who are suffering from a terrible drought.

G·28

BILL PICKETT

First Black Rodeo Star

by Sibyl Hancock

Early one morning before the sun came up, Bill Pickett tiptoed out of the back door of his house. His mother and father and little brother were still asleep. Bill was not sleepy. He was worried about a little colt.

Hurrying across the field, he let himself into the barn. The colt was lying in a bed of soft hay. Bill touched the colt. It did not feel hot any more.

"Little horse, here is some water," Bill said. He smiled when it drank every drop. "That's good," he said. "You're going to get well now."

Bill could hardly wait to tell his family the good news. He had helped take care of the colt for days. He felt proud. This was not the first time he had taken care of a sick animal. Everyone said that even though he was only a boy, he was good with animals.

Bill Pickett was born in 1860 on a ranch near Taylor, Texas. Bill's father worked on the ranch. He was one of many African American cowboys in the West. Bill's father liked being a cowboy. He knew how to handle horses and cattle and how to get along with people.

The ranch was big. Bill always had a lot of room to run and play. He worked too. He helped his mother hoe and weed the garden behind their small house.

One day when his chores were finished, Bill and his little brother ran over to the corral to watch their father and the other cowboys riding wild horses. The corral was a large pen enclosed by a circle of wooden fence. "Hurray!" Bill shouted. "Look at that horse trying to throw Pa off its back! That's what I want to do some day."

"Not me," his brother said. "You couldn't catch me on a bucking horse."

"Well, I'm going to learn how to ride bucking horses until they're broken," Bill said. "They will be as tame as lambs when I get through."

Bill didn't change his mind about wanting to work on a ranch. When he was about fifteen, he began to ride with the cowboys as they herded cattle. It took many weeks to drive cattle from the ranches to the towns, where they were sold.

After his first trail ride, Bill came home dusty and tired. "How do you like being a cowboy?" his mother asked him.

"I like it fine," Bill said. "But it's sure not as easy as I thought. Sometimes it rained, and I got all wet. Then other times the wind blew dust so thick I could hardly see."

"Were there any snakes?" she asked.

"Oh, yes," he said. "Big rattlesnakes! And at night when we were sleeping, I could hear coyotes howling."

As he grew older, Bill found jobs that took him away from home. He wandered across southern Texas and into Mexico. For a while he worked on ranches as far away as South America. He drove cattle through valleys and over hills. He helped men brand or burn a mark into the hides of their cattle. Each ranch had its own brand, so it was easy to know where the cattle belonged. Bill became skilled at roping calves that strayed from

their mothers. And once he had to use his gun to kill a mountain lion that was ready to jump on him. He was quick with a gun and nearly always hit his target.

After a time Bill grew tired of drifting from town to town and country to country. He never had a chance to make many friends, and he was lonely. He wanted to settle down in one place and stay. Bill came back to Texas. One day when he was herding cattle into a corral, Bill saw a tall man watching him. "I like the way you handle a horse," the man said. "My name is Colonel Zack Miller."

"I'm Bill Pickett," Bill said, shaking Colonel Zack's hand.

"I own the 101 Ranch in Oklahoma," Colonel Zack said. "How would you like to work for me?"

"I'd be pleased to work at your ranch," Bill said.

Bill had been a cowboy for a long time when he moved to the 101 Ranch. He had seen many ranches, but never one as huge as the 101. Colonel Zack and his brothers had turned the 101 into a regular little town. There was a post office, a school, and a general store. There were even churches, drugstores, and gas stations. The 101 Ranch was famous. People came from all over the country to visit it.

Bill felt at home on the 101 Ranch. He soon made friends with the other cowboys. One of his best friends was named Ted. For the first time in many years, he was not lonely.

Ted and Bill were working with some horses one day when they heard a colt scream with pain. Bill quickly found the little horse.

"What is the matter with him?" Ted asked.

"He's got a big splinter in his chest," Bill said. "I'll have to get it out."

"Let me help," Ted said. Ted held the little horse still while Bill removed the splinter.

"It's going to be a long time before this colt will be well," Bill said.

For weeks Bill nursed the colt back to health. One day the colt seemed almost well. "Come on, fellow, walk to me," Bill whispered. The colt tried to stand, and his legs wobbled and spread apart. Bill laughed. "I think your name should be Spradley!"

Bill visited Spradley every day and always had a lump of sugar for him to eat. As the colt grew older, Bill often took him into wide fields and let him run and kick. Spradley was becoming a strong and beautiful horse.

"Spradley looks great," Ted said. "Thanks to Bill's care."

"He sure does," Colonel Zack agreed. He motioned for Bill to come out of the corral. "Well, Bill, how would you like to have Spradley for your own horse?" Colonel Zack asked.

"My own horse?" Bill asked. "I can't believe it. Thank you, Colonel Zack. Did you hear that, Ted?" Bill said. "Spradley's *mine*."

Ted smiled. "I heard."

Bill had never been happier. He dearly loved Spradley. Bill taught him how to ride beside cattle and how to avoid their sharp horns. When Bill roped a calf, Spradley learned to back away so that the rope would be tight and the calf could not escape.

When Spradley was grown, he was a very good cowpony. He knew just how to help Bill herd the cattle.

One hot summer day Bill rode after a steer that had broken loose from the herd. He tried again and again to rope it, but he always missed. "Come on, Spradley, let's get him," Bill said. Spradley galloped close to the steer, and Bill leaped out of his saddle. He grabbed the old steer's horns with both hands and twisted its head sideways.

The steer rolled over on the ground.

Colonel Zack watched and shouted to the men nearby. "Come here! See what Bill did! He threw that steer just like a bulldog does!"

Everyone knew that a bulldog barked and snapped at stubborn cattle. If that did not work, the dog would bite the steer's nose and pull the animal down. But no one had ever seen a man throw a steer using only his hands.

"Do it again," Colonel Zack asked.

Bill grinned. "I sure will," he said. And he quickly bulldogged another steer.

"You've got to teach me how to do that," Ted told him.

"Me too," another cowboy said.

Soon all the cowboys wanted to learn how to wrestle a steer to the ground. But not many of them could do it. Only very strong and brave men could bulldog cattle.

It was not long before cowboys from nearby ranches came to the 101 Ranch to see who could bulldog a steer the quickest. The winner went home with a pocketful of money.

"You and Spradley really started something," Ted said. He leaned against the corral gate.

"I guess we did," Bill said. "I've never had so much money to spend."

One day Colonel Zack walked over to Bill and said, "More and more people are visiting the 101 Ranch to watch you fellows perform. I think I'm going to start giving a Wild West Show. I'll make it the best rodeo anyone ever saw. We can have elephants, camels, and buffalo.

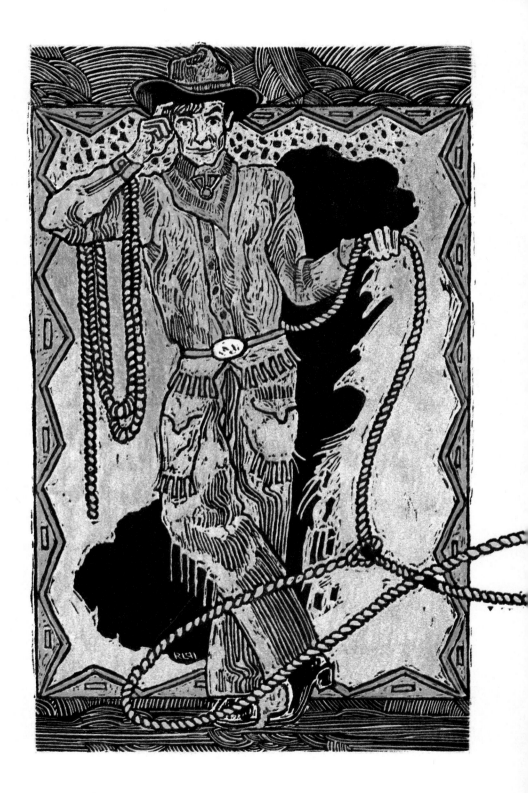

G·38

Maybe even some mules and long-horned steers and bears. Would you do your bulldogging act?"

"That would be fun," Bill said. "Can I use Spradley?"

"Sure," Colonel Zack said.

"I don't believe any rodeo has ever had a bulldogger," Ted said. "Bill will be the first."

When the rodeo opened, there were many cowboys in it besides Bill. Another of Bill's good friends, Will Rogers, was in the show. Will could do rope tricks better than just about anyone else. And he told jokes that made people laugh.

A group of newspapermen came to the 101 Ranch to see the Wild West Show. When Bill bulldogged a steer, the crowd clapped and cheered him. His name was printed in newspapers all over the country.

Being in a rodeo was dangerous. Cowboys took great chances when they worked with wild horses and cattle. The people watching the Wild West Show were frightened but excited by the danger.

Spradley traveled everywhere with Bill. The 101 rodeo went to Madison Square Garden in New York City.

Bill rode Spradley into the arena after a steer, and Will Rogers rode nearby. The steer suddenly jumped over a gate and landed right in the crowd. Nobody was hurt, but the people were scared. "Hey, Spradley," Bill shouted. "Let's get that steer!"

"I'm right behind you, Bill!" Will Rogers yelled.

Bill leaped from Spradley and grabbed the steer's horns. "I've got you now, old critter," Bill said. Will Rogers roped the animal's hind legs. He pulled the steer down into the arena with Bill holding onto the horns. No one in New York had ever seen such an exciting show. They thought the Wild West Show was wonderful.

Bill visited many cities. Everywhere he went people cheered him.

"How does it feel to be the star performer of the rodeo?" Ted asked one afternoon.

Bill smiled. "Aw—I'm no star. I just like bulldogging. Come on, let's go help load the animals." Ted and Bill walked to the long line of railroad cars that belonged to the Wild West Show. The rodeo was getting ready to leave for another town. "Six hundred animals in all," Bill said. "It's no wonder we have to have so many railroad cars."

"It's kind of hard to believe we can all travel together and so far," Ted said.

Bill let out a whistle. "Look at those elephants. I never get tired of watching them." He was happy in the great Wild West Show.

Thinking About It

1. Bill Pickett had many adventures, from traveling to South America to performing in the Wild West Show. Of all the things Bill did in his lifetime, which ones would you like to try?

2. The cowboys in the Wild West Show could ride bucking horses, lasso cattle, and bulldog steers. How might these "tricks" have helped the cowboys in their work back at the ranch?

3. Spradley, Bill Pickett's horse, has learned how to talk. What does he tell you about his life with Pickett?

Rose Johnson '91

Nature Rhymes

Rimas sobre la naturaleza

by Frances Alexander

1
Watch the sun sail
Eating its snail,
Throwing the peelings
Over the trail.

1
Allá está el sol
comiendo su caracol
y echando las cáscaras
a su labor.

2
There is the star
Eating its tar,
Throwing the scraps
Into a jar.

2
Allá está la estrella
comiendo su brea
y echando las cáscaras
a su botella.

3
Come see the moon
Eat her cactus prune,
Throwing the peelings
In the lagoon.

3
Allá está la luna
comiendo su tuna
y echando las cáscaras
a la laguna.

Christmas Tamales

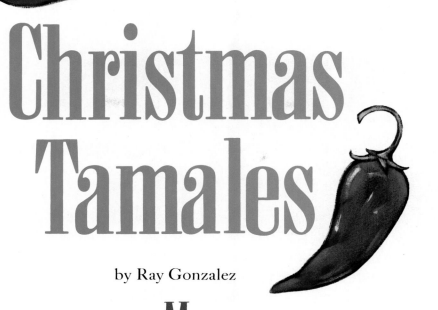

by Ray Gonzalez

My mother, Beatriz, is the best tamale maker in El Paso. The dozens of tamales she and her helpers produce during the Christmas holidays are an important part of an old Mexican tradition. The steaming masa pies are filled with delicious pork and red-hot chili. When rolled out of their corn-husk blankets, the tamales are like little bundles of joy.

Let me tell you about the Christmas of 1986, when I helped make tamales for the first time. Most tamale lovers don't realize how much effort goes into making tamales. They just like to peel off the steaming hojas and eat. When I helped out, I learned to appreciate the art of tamale making.

The most important ingredient for tamales is masa, or corn flour. The texture must be right, or the tamales will not turn out properly. Finding good masa in El Paso is not easy. The best masa comes from a tiendita, a grocery store, in the barrio.

My Aunt Consuelo and I went to a tiendita that was no larger than a city bus. When we entered the little shop, right away I could smell the musky scent of the masa. A woman behind the counter took our order and ran the masa through a corn meal grinder called a molino.

The masa rolled out of the molino in thick, heavy chunks made from ground meal and water. The mixture reminded me of wet cement. The woman packed the masa in butcher paper. We paid twenty dollars, knowing we'd bought the best masa that could be found.

My mother says corn meal spoils easily. So after we brought the masa home, she cooled it immediately and dumped it into the tina, a large metal tub.

After she added salt, melted lard, and baking powder, the masa had to be kneaded into the proper texture. My three younger sisters, Pat, Susy, and Sylvia, voted to give me the job. Kneading turned out to be my favorite part of making tamales. My family believes the special flavor of the tamales comes from the toiling palms of the tamale maker, which seem to add a natural spice to the recipe. We call this spice "la familia."

There I stood before the huge tub of thick, gooey stuff and sank my hands into it. The masa felt like grainy sand or the mud pies I made as a child. I kneaded the hard balls of masa into a smooth texture. I put all my weight into kneading. I grabbed, pinched, and squeezed. My sisters cheered, "Come on, Ray, you can do it. Look, Mom, we should have had Ray help us years ago!"

Sinking my fingers into the masa, I uncovered ball after ball of unkneaded dough. I churned the masa for more than half an hour until the dough turned light and fluffy. The fluffiness signals the next, and slowest, step: painting corn husks with the masa.

The final test to see if the masa is ready for the hojas comes from an old folk tradition. My mother took a glass of water, dipped a spoon into the masa, and dropped a tiny ball of masa into the glass. The masa floated to the top. She nodded and told me the floating masa means it is ready to go into the hojas. If the masa sinks, it must be kneaded some more.

The hojas are old, dried husks. Spreading the masa onto the husks takes hours. My sisters and I cleared the kitchen table and covered it with newspapers to collect the dripping masa. Then we all sat around the table, grabbed a stack of husks, and began to cover them with masa. We each dipped a spoon into the tub and spread the masa evenly onto the open husks.

Somehow, I got to know my sisters a little better that day. They had a lot of fun making jokes about my first experience tamale making. "You hold the hoja in your left hand and spread with your right," Susy laughed, when my first hoja slipped from my hands onto the floor with a splat.

After two spoonfuls of masa covered each husk, my mother and aunt spread a large spoonful of red-hot chili onto the masa surface. (The red chili had been cooked earlier with thick cubes of pork in giant vats.)

After we filled the husks with masa and chili, we folded each tamale carefully so nothing would fall out while they were being cooked.

Finally, we steamed the tamales for an hour and a half. We placed the little bundles, a couple of dozen at a time, in a pressure cooker, stacked carefully in a basket holder.

My mother says the same person who sets the tamales into the steamer must take them out when they are done. If anyone interferes with another person's batch, the tamales will not come out right. She guarded every batch of tamales as it cooked.

The unforgettable Christmas feast we had that year included the tamales I helped make. I could feel the weight of the masa in my stomach for days afterwards, but that was a small price to pay for sharing in a special family tradition.

Thinking About It

1. You are invited to the Gonzalez house to help the family make Christmas tamales. Tell about your experience.

2. You and a friend are eating tamales together. Your friend asks, "I wonder how tamales are made, and what ingredients are in them?" Explain tamale making to your friend.

3. The Gonzalez family cooks tamales together. Maybe you cook something with your family, or perhaps you cook something by yourself. Tell a story about preparing your favorite food.

The Best Town in the World

by Byrd Baylor

All my life I've heard about
a little, dirt-road,
one-store,
country town
not far from a rocky canyon
way back
in the Texas hills.

This town had lots of space
around it
with caves to find
and honey trees
and giant rocks to climb.

*I*t had a creek
and there were panther tracks
to follow
and you could swing
on the wild grapevines.
My father said it was
the best town in the world
and he just happened
to be born there.
How's that for being
lucky?

We always liked
to hear about
that town
where everything was
perfect.

Of course it had a name
but people called the town
and all the ranches
and the farms around it
just *The Canyon*,
and they called each other
Canyon People.

The way my father said it,
you could tell
it was a special thing
to be
one of those people.

All the best cooks
in the world lived there.
My father said
if you were walking down the road,
just hunting arrowheads
or maybe coming home from school,
they'd call you in
and give you
sweet potato pie
or gingerbread
and stand there
by the big wood stove
and smile at you
while you were eating.

It was that kind
of town.

The best blackberries
in the world
grew wild.

My father says
the ones in stores
don't taste a thing
like those
he used to pick.
Those tasted just like
a blackberry should.

He'd crawl into
    a tangle
    of blackberry thicket
    and eat all he wanted
    and finally
    walk home
    swinging his bucket
    (with enough for four pies)
    and his hands
    and his face
    and his hard bare feet
    would be stained
    that beautiful color.

    All plants
    liked
    to grow there.
    The town was famous for
    red chiles
    and for melons
    and for sweet corn, too.

    And it's a well-known fact
    that chickens in that canyon
    laid prettier brown eggs
    than chickens
    twenty miles on down the road.

    My father says
    no scientist
    has figured out
    why.

The dogs were smarter there.
They helped you herd the goats
and growled at rattlesnakes
before you even saw them.
And if you stopped
to climb a tree
your dogs stopped, too.
They curled up and waited
for you to come down.
They didn't run off
by themselves.

Summer days
were longer there
than they are
in other places,
and wildflowers grew taller
and thicker on the hills—
not just the yellow ones.
There were all shades of
lavender and purple
and orange and red
and blue
and the palest kind of pink.
They all had butterflies
to match.

Fireflies lit up
the whole place
at night,
and in the distance
you could hear
somebody's fiddle
or banjo
or harp.

My father says
no city water
ever tasted half as good
as water that he carried
in a bucket from the well
by their back door.

And there isn't
any water
anywhere
as clear
as the water
in that ice cold creek
where all the children swam.
You could look down
and see the white sand
and watch the minnows
flashing by.

*B*ut
when my father came to the part
about that ice cold water
we would always say,
"It doesn't sound
so perfect
if the water was
ice cold."

He'd look surprised
and say,
"But that's the way
creek water
is supposed to be—
ice cold."

So we learned that
however
things were
in that town
is just exactly how
things *ought* to be.

People there
did things
in their own way.
For instance—
spelling.

Sometimes I'd be
surprised
at how my father
spelled a word
that I'd already learned
at school,
but if I mentioned it,
he'd say,
"The way I spell it
is the way
they spelled it
there,
so it must be right."

But my mother said
since we weren't living
there,
maybe we should just
go ahead
and spell the way
they do in other places.
So we did,
though we always liked
his way.

Maybe that's part of the reason
it was the best town
in the world.
You could do things
whatever way
seemed good
to you.

*F*or instance, in the summertime
when the air was full of birdsong
and cicadas,
my father
(when he was little
and even when he was big)
liked to take his supper
and climb up in a tree
and eat it there
alone.

He did it almost every night.
He had thick slices
of his mother's homemade bread
in a bowl of milk,
fresh from the evening milking.

No one ever said,
"Eat something else,"
and no one ever said,
"Don't eat it in a tree."
If someone, walking by,
glanced up and saw him
with his bowl and spoon,
they wouldn't say a thing
except,
"Good evening, George."

Of course you knew
everyone's name
and everyone
knew
yours.

For his birthday
every year
my father had
a cake
and a birthday song
and a nickel in his hand
to spend.

He'd jump on his horse,
Doodlebug,
and ride off
as fast as he could,
stirring up dust
all the way
to Mr. Patterson's store.

He always bought
a nickel's worth
of candy.

"It doesn't seem like much,"
we'd say.

He'd say,
"Remember,
this was not just
any candy.
This was the best
in the world."

There was a bin of it.
Sometimes
he'd stand there
half the morning,
choosing
five pieces
while everybody gave him
good advice.

He says
he never did
choose *wrong*.
He still remembers
how that candy
used to taste.

People in that town
liked any kind of
celebration.

The best speeches
in the world
were made right there
on Texas Independence Day
and July Fourth.

And every Sunday
people from the farms
and ranches
came to town
with wagons full of children
and baskets full of food.

After church,
the whole town gathered
at long tables
underneath the tall shade trees
where all those famous cooks
were bringing out
their famous food.

You could count on fried chicken
and chile con carne
and black-eyed peas
and corn on the cob
and corn bread sticks
and biscuits
and frijoles
and squash and turnip greens
and watermelon pickles
and dumplings
and fritters
and stews.

There was another whole table
just for desserts.
Sometimes you'd see
five different kinds of
chocolate cake.

My father said
he thought that if
he took just one
he'd hurt the feelings of
four other
chocolate cake cooks—
so he took one
of each.
But then he thought
that if they saw him
eating cake
he'd hurt the feelings of
the pie cooks,
so he ate pie, too—
to be polite.

He said
he was famous
for being polite
to the cooks.

It seemed like
everybody
in that town
was famous.
My father said
it was because
the smartest people
in the world
were
all
right there.

We asked him
what they did
that was so smart.
He said,
"They all had sense enough
to know the best town
in the world
when they saw it.
That's smart."

And they were smart
in other ways.

For instance,
they could tell time
without wearing a watch.
They just glanced
at the sun
and they *knew*.
They wouldn't be more
than ten minutes off...
and ten minutes off
doesn't matter.

They could tell
by the stars
what the weather would be.
They could tell
by the moon
when to plant.

If they needed
a house
or corral
or a barn,
they didn't pay someone
to come build it for them.
They cut their own trees
and found their own rocks
and dug their own earth.

Then,
whatever it was,
they built it to last
for a hundred years—
and it did.

Suppose
their children
wanted
kites
or jump ropes
or whistles
or stilts...

They didn't have to
go to stores
and buy just what
was there.

They knew how to make
the best toys
in the world.

On winter nights
when they were
sitting by the fire,
by lamplight,
talking,
you'd see them
making
bows and arrows
or soft rag dolls
or blocks
or tops
or bamboo flutes
or even a checkerboard
carved out of oak.

My father said
sometimes
they'd let you
paint the checkers
red
or black
and you'd be
proud.

We liked everything
we ever heard
about those people
and that town,
but we always
had to ask:
"If it really was

the best town
in the world,
why weren't
more people
there?"

And he would say,
"Because
if a lot
of people
lived there,
it wouldn't be
the best town
anymore.
The best town
can't
be crowded."

We always wished
that we could live there
and be
Canyon People, too.

Still,
we used to wonder
if possibly,
just *possibly*,
there might be
another
perfect town
somewhere.

To find out,
I guess
you'd have to follow
a lot of
dirt roads
past
a whole lot of
wildflower hills.

I guess
you'd have to
try
a lot of
ice cold
swimming holes
and eat
a lot of
chocolate cake
and pat
a lot of dogs.

It seems
like a good thing
to do.

Thinking About It

1. You are visiting a friend who lives in the town described in *The Best Town in the World*. While you're there, how will you spend your time?

2. Find your favorite part of the story. Tell it to someone in your own words. Try to use your voice to express the mood, or feeling, of the part you choose.

3. What if this story were about the place where you live? What things could the story include?

An Interview With The Chinese Texans

by Marian L. Martinello
and William T. Field, Jr.

What do you think the term "Chinese Texan" means to most people?

If people don't know us very well, they probably think of railroads, laundries, and Chinese food.

Why?

Well, most of the first Chinese who came to live in Texas came here as railroad construction workers. Later, many of those people started laundries and restaurants. Those restaurants served meat-and-potatoes-type dishes in the early days because that's what other Americans liked. Today, the special flavors of Chinese foods like sweet-and-sour pork and chicken, dried fish, and rice are enjoyed by many Americans. That's interesting, because young Chinese Texans, especially, eat typical American foods more often than Chinese foods.

Is there a type of Chinese food that is particularly well known to Americans?

Chop suey! But that is not really Chinese food. It is a Chinese-American dish. It was "invented" in this country. Chop suey is almost unknown to Chinese people who live in China.

Do Chinese Texans have any special traditions?

Yes, we still enjoy the traditions our Chinese ancestors brought to Texas. You can tell an invitation to a Chinese party or special event by gold engraving on red paper. Red is a special color to Chinese.

During weddings, the bride is dressed in the typical white gown that most American brides wear. She is also given jade and gold family heirlooms.

A Chinese Texan bride and groom usually have a tea ceremony that honors the parents of the groom during the wedding reception. The two families exchange moon cakes and Chinese pastries.

Once in a while, we have a "red egg" party. This is held when a baby is one month old. The baby's head is rubbed with a red-colored egg, and red eggs are given to guests as party favors.

We also have "long life" parties for our parents. Chinese Texans still believe, as their ancestors did, that parents and older people should be respected. A special birthday celebration is held for a parent's 60th, 70th, or 80th birthday. Guests receive chopsticks and a rice bowl inscribed with the Chinese character "long life."

Why is the color red so important to Chinese Texans?

Red means good luck and happiness to all Chinese. If you ever attend a Chinese New Year celebration, you'll see the color red on many things and in many places.

What's the Chinese New Year celebration like?

You really have to see one to enjoy it. The Chinese Lunar New Year is held each year. It is a time to feast and have fun.

In big cities like San Francisco and New York, there is a parade to celebrate the New Year. Big papier-mâché dragons and lions are traditional parts of the parade. The King Lung is a huge dragon that is paraded through the streets. It has always been a traditional part of Chinese holidays and special events—even funerals. The King Lung means both joy and sorrow, so it becomes part of both our happy and our sad times.

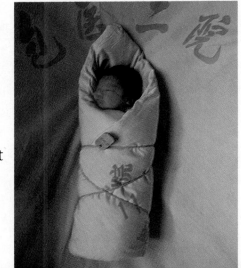

Chinese New Year is a time to start again just as January 1 is for the Western world. We Chinese Americans have two New Years—the one most Americans celebrate on January 1 and our own, which is usually held near the end of January or in early February. The Lunar New Year is a time to pay off debts and start the new year with a clean slate. On New Year's Eve, many Chinese families have a special dinner and stay up until midnight to wish one another a happy new year. Parents often give their children gifts of small amounts of money in red envelopes. We also explode firecrackers.

Many Americans don't know that the firecrackers exploded on the Fourth of July were introduced by the Chinese in San Francisco when they celebrated the admission of California to the United States in 1850.

What do Chinese Texans wear?

The clothing we wear is like the clothing other Americans wear. On special occasions, women still sometimes put on the *chipao*, a pretty and very comfortable type of dress that is still worn in China.

Many years ago, the Chinese who worked on the railroads wore the traditional Chinese clothing of white cotton blouses and wide pants. The men grew their hair long enough to make it into a braid that hung down their backs. They also wore large straw hats to protect their heads from the hot Texas sun. They really stood out from the other railroad workers. But things have changed since then. If you tried to pick out Chinese Texans from other Texans by the clothing they wear, you'd never find them.

Would you be able to find Chinese Texans by the places they live or where they go to church?

When they first settled in Texas cities, Chinese Texans tended to live in the same neighborhoods. But the only city that had a Chinatown was El Paso, and that did not last to this day. There are no longer special neighborhoods in Texas cities where Chinese live together.

Most Chinese Texans are Christians. When the railroad construction workers settled in Texas, Protestant and Catholic

churches helped them. A Baptist Chinese mission in El Paso was helping the new settlers in 1896. In San Antonio, too, the Chinese Baptist Church was started. It still has services in English and Chinese. The same is true in Houston, where the Chinese Baptist Church and Grace Chapel offer Chinese Texans places to worship in the Chinese language.

Chinese Texans have worked hard to become recognized citizens of the United States and the state of Texas. They have not had an easy time. For many years, especially during the early part of their history here, Chinese people were not accepted by others. But their respect for one another, for family tradition, and for the communities they joined caused them to be law-abiding, respectable citizens.

The Chinese brought to Texas a way of life, customs, and traditions that have blended with those of other groups of people who live in the state. Chinese Texans are much more than Chinese people who happen to live in Texas. Their history is a part of Texas history. Their culture is part of Texas culture.

Thinking About It

1. Be the interviewer in this article. What other questions do you ask the Chinese Texans?

2. You have just come from China to visit relatives in Texas. What surprises you about Texas and the Chinese Texans?

3. If you were going to live in a new country, which three customs would you most like to bring with you? Why?

Frost Flowers

by Ilo Hiller

On that first really cold morning of the year when the air is crisp and temperatures hover below freezing, if you happen to be strolling in the woods or near a creek where the frostweed grows, you may get to see nature's unusual ice sculptures, the frost flowers.

Looking like spun glass or cotton candy, these fragile creations, which are really not flowers at all, last only until the warm rays of the morning sun melt them away. Since their formation and disappearance cover such a short period of time each year, few people have seen them or even know of their existence.

Frost flowers develop when air temperatures are freezing but the ground still is warm enough for the plant's root system to be active. Plant juices flow from these roots up into the stem, where the cold air freezes them. As the moisture in the plant freezes, the ice crystals push out through the stem. They may emerge from a small slit to form thin, ribbonlike strands or they may split open a whole section of the stem and push out in a thin, curling sheet. Sometimes several ribbons of ice push out to create a flowerlike petal effect. As long as the juices flow, air temperatures remain low, and the plant is shaded from the sun, these ice crystals continue to form.

Only a few species of plants are capable of producing these icy creations. The frostweed, *Verbesinia virginica*, which commonly occurs in Texas, is one of them. These waist- to shoulder-high plants grow in dense patches in the moist, shaded soil of river or creek bottoms and form heavy undergrowths in the shade of large trees. This plant also is known as Indian tobacco and tickweed because the dried leaves were once used by Indians as tobacco and people walking through the plants invariably gather a few seed ticks.

If you want to enjoy the frost flowers in person this year, locate some of the frostweed plants before

cold weather arrives. Then, early on that first really cold morning when the temperatures dip below freezing, go back to see if frost flowers are "blooming." Take along your camera and some flashbulbs so you can share your frost flowers with others who don't get a chance to see them. Be sure to go early, because they'll probably be gone by nine.

Thinking About It

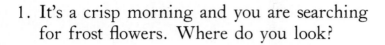

1. It's a crisp morning and you are searching for frost flowers. Where do you look?

2. A young child says to you, "What's a frost flower?" How do you explain what a frost flower is?

3. Frost flowers aren't really flowers. Think of another name for frost flowers, and tell why the name would be a good one.

Visiting Huelo y Huela

by
Marisa Perales

As I walk up the sidewalk to the small, wooden house surrounded by beautiful, colorful flowers, my grandparents are already waiting for my family and me on the front porch. "Hi, *Huelo* and *Huela*," I say as I embrace my grandmother first, then my grandfather, giving each of them a peck on the cheek. "Hi, *mija!*" they respond. My grandmother, a pleasantly plump woman in her mid-sixties with short gray hair,

gently pats my behind as she hurries me along inside the house.

The interior of the house is decorated with pictures of grandchildren everywhere. While sitting on the worn couch covered with crocheted furniture covers, I spot the large picture of myself in a *quinceañera* dress on the opposite wall. The picture brings back many pleasant memories of that special day when I turned fifteen. It represented the day that I entered maturity and womanhood. I remember the traditional Mass and the beautiful Spanish music sung by the choir. Afterwards, my friends, my family, and I celebrated at a festively decorated dance hall. We danced to the Spanish music of a live band. It was such a memorable evening!

"Food's ready!" My grandmother's loud voice brings me back to the present. As I approach the kitchen, a pleasant aroma greets me. "Mmm," I say, "what did you make for lunch, *Huela?*" *"Arroz con pollo y tortillas,"* she replies. "Oh, I just love chicken and rice." We all gather around the kitchen table with the vinyl table cover to say a customary prayer before we eat. My father recites a short prayer in Spanish that I do not completely understand. We then sit down to eat off of the plastic plates that do not all match and drink tea from glasses of different sizes. The picture of the Last Supper adorns the main wall of the eating area. My parents and grandparents

 make casual conversation entirely in Spanish while we eat. My grandfather asks how I'm doing in school, and I see his face beam with pride as I tell him I made the honor roll. He pulls a dollar bill out of his pocket and hands it to me as a small reward. I first refuse, telling him, "No, really, I can't accept it." However, after enough persuasion, I gratefully accept it and give him an affectionate hug in return. Although a dollar may not seem like much, I know it comes from the heart.

My parents have returned to the living area where my grandfather has turned on the old radio to a Spanish station. My grandmother has put on her floral-print apron over her loose-fitting dress and has begun to wash the dishes while I just stand and stare out the back-door window. I giggle softly to myself as I see the striped boxer shorts hanging out on the clothesline. When I think about it, I realize if my mother hung our underwear and clothes outside, I'd be terribly embarrassed. I also realize we hardly ever listen to Spanish music at home, and I would be thoroughly humiliated if my mother placed covers over our furniture. However, it doesn't seem unusual to see these things here at my grandparents' house.

Although the traditional Hispanic customs are disappearing in today's society, the values and the morals that my grandparents and parents have taught me will continue to live through my

children. My parents, who are both successful, have raised me in a home where Spanish is seldom spoken, but it is always appreciated and respected. Both my parents were brought up in a home where not much more was offered than food to eat and a warm place to sleep, but there was always an abundance of love. It was a home in which religion and education were highly regarded. All of these Hispanic customs and morals that I value so much represent what being Hispanic means to me. These are the things that make me a truly unique individual.

"Honey, are you ready to leave?" I hear my mother ask. "Oh, yes, I am," I respond as I drift back to reality. While standing in the front doorway ready to leave, I feel the love pour out of each of my grandparents when we embrace. Again I kiss each of them and say, *"Adios! Te amo Huelo y Huela.* I love you!" as I slowly head toward the car.

Thinking About It

1. Your friend Marisa Perales invites you to join her on a visit to her grandparents. What do you remember best about the visit?

2. Marisa writes of some Hispanic customs inherited from her grandparents that her mother and father have not changed. What are they?

3. You are Marisa's grandparent. You have just finished reading Marisa's essay. What do you think about it?

A WRITER IN

TEXAS

by Joan Lowery Nixon

Writers can write anywhere. I have written in planes, on trains, on ships, in taxis, and while traveling in a bus across New Zealand. I've written in hotels and motels throughout the United States and in homes in California, Montana, and Texas.

But there's something special about being a writer in Texas.

We know the facts about Texas: It's the second largest state in the United States; it has deserts and forests, mountains and swamps, a national seashore, a national park, and a great many historical museums, forts, universities, art galleries, cities, and towns.

That's all well and good, but what makes Texas really special for a writer? Could it be a mixture of history and mystery?

Many years ago, countless merchant sailing ships and pirate ships were shipwrecked along the Texas coast, and parts of their contents washed ashore. Sometimes, after a storm, the Padre Island sand that covered them for so long blows away, exposing rotted, wooden hulks of sailing ships, ancient pistols, and gold and silver coins—real finds for treasure hunters. But what about writers searching for ideas?

Supposedly, other treasures lie buried near the sea. There are many legends about the notorious Jean Laffite and other pirates who plundered ships which had been heading for New Orleans. The pirates sailed to the then-uninhabited Padre Island to hide their stolen gold and jewels.

How does someone hide treasure in sand dunes and find it again after the dunes have been moved by the winds and tides? It's difficult, especially when such landmarks as trees, stakes, or sheds have blown away. Just think of all the treasure that may be hidden still! The beginning of a story idea?

Or are stories sparked by ghosts? Texas is a great place for ghosts. Mysterious ghost lights have appeared for over one hundred years in the small West Texas mountain town of Marfa. In the East Texas big thicket country the strange Saratoga Light zooms up and down the deserted Old Bragg Road, only to disappear. And near Fredericksburg, in the hill country, a state park has been named for an enchanted rock. On this five-hundred-foot high granite dome, American Indians once claimed to see ghost fires after dark. On many summer nights the rock creaks and groans, but geologists claim it's just the sound of the rock contracting. Ghosts or not? Who knows?

No sounds come from the rocks which hold the dinosaur footprints along the river in Glen Rose. It's quiet country, so quiet that we can stand in the massive prints, close our eyes, and imagine those fearsome creatures lumbering past us to get a drink. Can this be fuel for a writer?

Not all story inspirations come from mysteries. In Texas we can tour Palo Duro Canyon and deep canyons near Del Rio; explore caverns and caves near Georgetown, Sonora, and San Marcos; and swim in the Gulf of Mexico. We can ride in brightly painted barges down the San Antonio River, passing between the actors on the stage of the Arneson River Theater and the audience seated across the river. We can white-water raft down the Rio Grande in Big Bend, or we can float lazily in inner tubes down the shallow, shady Comal River near New Braunfels. Do story ideas come from the setting? the time? the place?

Texas has a great many working ranches and dude ranches with early morning outdoor "cowboy breakfasts," rides on horseback or in wagons, rodeos, and chili-cooking contests. In Texas we can attend the blessing of the fishing fleet at Brazosport or Galveston, watch the tribal dances on the Alabama-Coushatta Indian

Reservation, or carry a lighted candle and join
others in the Christmas songs at the festivals of
Las Posadas and Las Luminarias along the river
in San Antonio.

Why is it special to be a writer in Texas?
It's because anywhere in Texas we can meet
friendly, interesting people who have come to
our state from all over the world, bringing their
own customs and culture and beauty with them.
And people—to a writer—are the greatest
inspiration of all.

COAHUILA

G·98

THINKING

A B O U T I T

1. You are chatting with Joan Lowery Nixon, discussing possible topics for her next book. Based on what she has explained in this article, what will you suggest to her?

2. Texas inspires Joan Lowery Nixon to write stories. Find an inspiration she mentions in the selection, and tell why it could be a good subject for a story.

3. Be a Texas writer. First, decide on a topic. Then make up an exciting first sentence.

You Bet Your
Britches,
Claude

by Joan Lowery Nixon

Chapter One

It was early in the morning, with the sun as yellow and hot as the yolk of a just-fried egg, when Shirley, Claude, and their newly adopted son Tom arrived in town.

"There's too many people around here to suit me," Claude said. "I'm hankerin' to get back home and settle into some peace and quiet." He shook his head sadly. "Only lately we ain't had us much peace and quiet."

He hitched the pair of sway-backed horses to a post and added, "I'd be happier than a pig in a mud puddle if I could keep away all those wrong-minded folks who come by our farm."

Shirley patted Claude's shoulder. "I'll think of somethin'," she said. "We can head for home soon as I pick up a few things for Tom and collect my reward money for catchin' the bank robber."

"You get busy with the shoppin'," Claude said. "I'll find the sheriff and bring him back here."

The minute Claude was gone, Tom led Shirley across the street and into The Good Eats Cafe where his sister Bessie had been left with Mrs. Krumbly.

The only customers were a pair of cowboys who were chewing hard on what looked like beef stew. A little cinnamon-haired girl, not much bigger than a spring cricket, was on her hands and knees scrubbing the floor.

"Bessie!" Tom called.

Bessie threw the scrub brush into the air and leaped up to hug Tom.

"Tom!" she yelled. "Where'd you go? Whatcha doin' here? Who's that you're with?"

"Bessie," Tom said, soon as he'd managed to pry her loose, "meet Shirley, who's so kind and tenderhearted that she's goin' to be our new mother."

"Oh no, she's not!" Mrs. Krumbly waddled out from the kitchen waving a big, drippy, stirrin' spoon. "That saucy, little, no-account, ragamuffin gal belongs to me!"

Well, Shirley never could stand to hear folks talk ugly, so she stepped up to Mrs. Krumbly, nose to nose, and said, "You got no call to bad-mouth Bessie. I'll pay you fair and square the twenty dollars you gave for her, but there's no two ways about it. Bessie is comin' with me."

Mrs. Krumbly made a grab for Bessie, but Bessie scooted around the scrub pail, sloshing water in Mrs. Krumbly's path. Mrs. Krumbly slipped and landed in the scrub pail where she stuck, kicking and waving her arms and legs like a beetle on its back.

"If anybody's gonna square things, it ought to be Mrs. Krumbly," Bessie shouted. "She's been hornswoggling her customers. First off, I spied her not given' 'em enough change."

"Bessie's always had sharp eyes," Tom said.

"And second," Bessie went on, "that so-called beef stew she makes has more little critters in it than beef."

The two cowboys leaped up from their chairs grabbing their throats and making terrible noises.

Just then Claude and the sheriff walked in.

Claude thought on what he saw. Then he said, "Shirley, you want to tell me how come those cowboys are hoppin' around like frogs on a hot rock and that cook lady is sittin' in a scrub pail?"

"*I'll* tell you! I'll tell you everything that happened," Bessie said eagerly. "It's a long story."

But before Bessie could say a single word, Shirley hushed her. "You bet your britches, Claude!" she said.

Chapter Two

The sheriff gave Shirley the fifty-dollar reward money for catching the bank robber. Before he took Mrs. Krumbly to jail he smiled at Bessie and said, "Little gal, you're as good as any legal, sworn-in deputy."

Shirley explained to Claude about Bessie, but Claude said, "Sister or no sister, there's no way to have peace and quiet with a chatty little eight-year-old gal in the house. You better find someone else to take her in, while I tend to the horses."

Shirley took Bessie in one hand and Tom in the other and headed to Dandee's Dry Goods Store. "First thing we're goin' to do is get some new clothes," Shirley said.

"But what's goin' to happen to Bessie?" Tom asked.

"Don't worry," Shirley said as they entered the store. "I'll think of somethin'."

Shirley bought Tom and Bessie each some shoes, striped suspenders for Tom, and a blue hair bow for Bessie. But all the while Bessie kept eyeing a tall, dusty cowboy who wandered through the store, his flat, empty saddlebags slung over his shoulder.

"I'll be with you soon," Mr. Dandee told the cowboy.

"No hurry," the cowboy said. "I'll just look around."

Shirley picked out underclothes and nightshirts, a petticoat for Bessie, a felt hat for Tom, and two cents worth of jellybeans. Then she asked to see some bolts of sturdy cotton.

"I'll be with you soon," Mr. Dandee called to the cowboy, who was at the back of the store.

"No hurry," the cowboy called back.

For Tom, Shirley picked out some dark brown twill that would wear well, and for Bessie, some soft blue cotton lawn just right for a cinnamon-haired little girl.

As Mr. Dandee began to measure out the goods, the cowboy hurried to the counter and laid down some change. "All I'm gettin' is this chawin' tobacco," he said and quick-like started toward the door.

But all of a sudden Bessie was in his way. She tugged at his bulging saddlebags and yelled for Shirley.

"Look out, you little nuisance!" the cowboy shouted.

Well, Shirley never could stand to hear folks talk ugly, so she stepped right up to the cowboy, nose to nose, and said, "You got no call to bad-mouth Bessie."

At that moment Bessie gave such a yank to the cowboy's saddlebags it pulled him off balance. Down he went, his saddlebags spilling out all the things he'd stolen from the store. A pair of red long johns lay stretched out across him.

Shirley rested a foot on the cowboy's stomach, in the middle of the red long johns, just in case he had a mistaken notion to move, while Mr. Dandee ran to find the sheriff.

Bessie shouted, "I spied that cowboy sneakin' all sorts of things into his saddlebags!"

"Bessie's always had sharp eyes," Tom said.

Just then Mr. Dandee, Claude, and the sheriff hurried into the store.

Claude thought on what he saw. Then he said, "Shirley, you want to tell me how come you stepped so hard on that man that he shot right out of his underwear?"

"I'll tell you! I'll tell you everything that happened," Bessie said eagerly. "It's a long, *long* story."

But before Bessie could say a single word, Shirley hushed her. "You bet your britches, Claude!" she said.

Chapter Three

"Little gal, you're as good as any legal, sworn-in deputy," the sheriff told Bessie before he took the cowboy off to jail.

Shirley put an arm around Bessie's shoulders and said, "Claude, let's talk about keepin' Bessie."

"Nope," Claude said. "There's no way to have peace and quiet with a chatty little gal in the house."

Shirley handed some money to Mr. Dandee and said to Claude, "If you'll tote my parcels to the wagon, I'll take the rest of my reward money to the bank for safe keeping."

She took Bessie in one hand and Tom in the other and hurried down the street to the bank.

"What's goin' to happen to Bessie?" Tom asked.

"Don't worry," Shirley said. "I'll think of somethin'."

Nobody but Mr. Pilly, the cashier, was in the bank, so Shirley went straight to the customer window. Tom stood polite-like off to one side, but Bessie clambered up to peer through the iron grille on top of the counter.

Mr. Pilly quickly snapped shut a large, black satchel and scowled at Shirley. "I've got no time for you now," he said. "I've got to catch the next stage."

"But I want to put my money in the bank," Shirley said. "Where's Mr. Witherspoon, the bank president?"

"He's home in bed," Mr. Pilly said. "How much money do you want to put in the bank?"

"Thirty dollars," Shirley said.

Mr. Pilly smiled the way a hungry rattlesnake smiles at a prairie dog and scribbled something on a piece of paper. "In that case, give me your money. Here's your receipt." He snatched

the bills, picked up his satchel, and strode to
the door.

But all of a sudden Bessie was in his way.
She tugged at his satchel and yelled for Shirley.

Mr. Pilly tugged back, shouting at Bessie.
"Get out of my way, you little raggletaggle,
trouble-making pest!"

Well, Shirley never could stand to hear folks
talk ugly, so she stepped right up to Mr. Pilly,
nose to nose, and said, "You got no call to bad-
mouth Bessie."

Bessie gave such a yank to Mr. Pilly's satchel
that he tumbled end over end down the steps,
pulling Shirley, Bessie, and the satchel with him.

Mr. Pilly landed face down with Shirley
sitting on top of him. The satchel broke open,
spilling money into Shirley's lap.

Bessie leaped to her feet and shouted, "I spied what was in that satchel afore Mr. Pilly closed it, and I figured he was fixin' to steal it!"

"Bessie's always had sharp eyes," Tom said.

Folks crowded around to see what was making such a commotion, and Claude and the sheriff came running.

Claude thought on what he saw. Then he said, "Shirley, you want to tell me how come you're sittin' on the bank cashier, countin' his money?"

"*I'll* tell you. I'll tell you everything that happened," Bessie said eagerly. "It's a long, long, *long* story."

But Shirley hushed her. She got up and said to the sheriff, "You said yourself that Bessie's as good as any legal, sworn-in deputy."

"Better," the sheriff said. "In all my days I've never seen anyone so quick at catchin' crooks."

"So why not make her a real, legal, sworn-in deputy?" Shirley asked.

The sheriff studied on it. "She's a mite young and small to be a deputy," he said.

"Look at it this way," Shirley said. "She can grow into the job."

"I guess that's right," the sheriff said. He took a tin star from his pocket and pinned it onto Bessie's dress. "Raise your right hand," he said.

As Bessie did, the sheriff, in a deep official-sounding voice said, "Under the rights given to me by the great state of Texas I hereby appoint this little gal Bessie an honest-to-goodness, everythin'-legal, sworn-in deputy. Bessie, you got somethin' to say in honor of the occasion?"

Bessie drew herself up as tall as she could and took a deep breath. "I'm right proud to be a deputy," she began.

But Shirley hushed her. "If we had a deputy livin' on our place," Shirley said to Claude, "the word would get out, and wrong-minded folks would steer clear."

"Makes sense to me," the sheriff said.

"And with no wrong-minded folks stoppin'
by, our home would be mighty peaceful and quiet,"
Shirley said.

"Bound to be," the sheriff said.

Claude thought on it a moment. Then he
smiled and said to Bessie, "Get in the wagon,
daughter."

He took Shirley's arm. "No reason why we
can't build *two* extra rooms onto the side of the
house," he told her.

Shirley's smile was so bright that some folks
around those parts got up and pulled down their
window shades. She took Bessie's hand and held it
tightly. "You bet your britches, Claude!" she said.

Thinking About It

1. You are a character in this story. Which one are you? Why?

2. Is *You Bet Your Britches, Claude* a tall tale, or could it really have happened? Why do you think so?

3. After Bessie went to live with Claude, Shirley, and Tom, the wacky family got mixed up in a new adventure. What was it?

Another Book by Joan Lowery Nixon
How did Claude and Shirley happen to meet each other in the first place? Find out the whole long, *long* story in *Fat Chance, Claude*.

G·116

Hey Little Girl

Collected by Barbara Michels
and Bettye White

Hey little girl with dippity do
Your mom's got the measles
And your daddy do too
Take a ABCDEFG
Take a HIJKLMNOP
Take a booster shot
Take a booster shot
And freeze

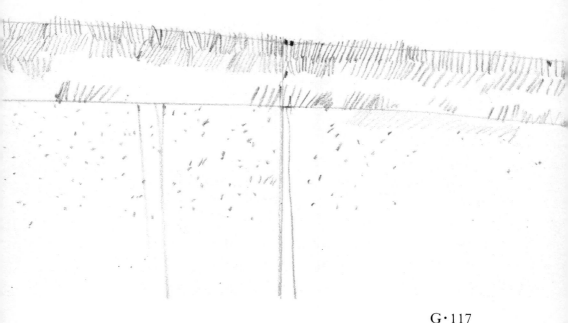

Miss Mary Mack

Collected by Barbara Michels
and Bettye White

Miss Mary Mack Mack Mack
All dressed in black black black
With silver buttons buttons buttons
All down her back back back
She asked her mother mother mother
For fifteen cents cents cents
To see the elephant elephant elephant
Jump the fence fence fence
He jumped so high high high
He touched the sky sky sky
And never came back
'Til the fourth of July-ly-ly

Old lady Dinah Dinah Dinah
Sick in the bed bed bed
Sent for the doctor doctor doctor
And the doctor said said said
Now get up Dinah Dinah Dinah
You ain't sick sick sick
All you need need need
Is a hickory stick stick stick

Uncle Ed Ed Ed
Fell out of bed bed bed
Bust his head head head
On a piece of corn bread bread bread
Corn bread rough rough rough
Biscuits tough tough tough
Never had enough-nough-nough
Of that good old stuff stuff stuff

July third third third
July fourth fourth fourth
July the eighth eighth eighth
A knife and a fork fork fork

1833-1907

ELISABET NEY

Artist Against All Odds

by Betsy Warren

lisabet stamped her foot and shouted.

"I *will* go to art school. No one can stop me."

Mrs. Ney looked at her daughter in astonishment. "It's impossible, Elisabet. Girls are not allowed in art classes here in Germany."

"And besides," said Mr. Ney, "you are seventeen years old. Soon you will marry. An education would be a waste of time."

Elisabet shook her head. "I will be a sculptor. My mind is made up."

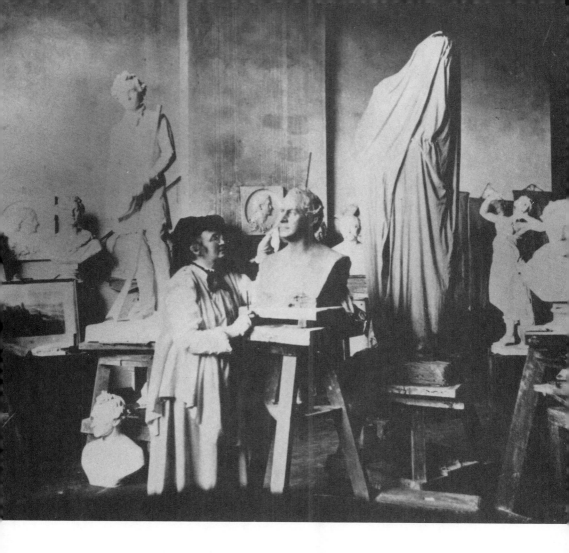

To her parents' dismay, Elisabet did become a sculptor. She was the first woman allowed to enter classes at the art academy in Munich, Germany. There she graduated at the top of her class and was given a scholarship to study in Berlin.

It was not long before everyone in Germany had heard about the remarkable young Miss Ney. She traveled all over Europe. Her works were entered in competitions. King George V and King Wilhelm of Prussia asked her to make statues of them.

n 1865 Elisabet married Edmund Montgomery, a doctor. But she would not let Edmund tell anyone they were married. She wanted to be sure that everyone would still call her Miss Ney. Even Edmund called her Miss Ney.

Elisabet and her husband wanted to get away from the wars being fought in Europe. In 1870 they came to the United States. After two years in Georgia, they moved to Hempstead, Texas. There they bought a large cotton plantation, Liendo.

Elisabet ran Liendo while her husband practiced medicine and wrote scientific articles. She directed the workers in planting and harvesting crops. There was no time for her sculpture, especially after two sons were born to the Montgomerys.

The women in Hempstead found Elisabet strange because she was so different from them. They wore their hair and their skirts very long. Elisabet cut her curly red hair short and wore loose gowns over purple woolen bloomers. And when her neighbors came to call, Elisabet served them buttermilk and dry toast instead of tea and cake.

Few people in Texas knew that Miss Ney had been a sculptor in Europe. The governor of Texas, Oran Roberts, knew of her though. In 1883 he asked Elisabet to give advice on the design of the new capitol that was being built in Austin.

At about the same time, Elisabet was asked to make statues of Sam Houston and Stephen F. Austin for the World's Fair to be held in Chicago.

Elisabet was fifty-nine years old and had done very little work as a sculptor in twenty years, but that did not stop her.

She moved to Austin and set up a workshop in the basement of the capitol.

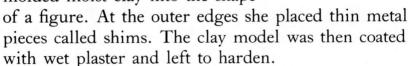

lisabet had not forgotten the steps to take for making a piece of sculpture. After drawing the subject, she formed a small doll-size model with clay. When she was satisfied with it, she then made a heavy wire support of the height she wished the finished statue to be. Around the wire, called an armature, she molded moist clay into the shape of a figure. At the outer edges she placed thin metal pieces called shims. The clay model was then coated with wet plaster and left to harden.

The dried mold was pried apart at the seam made by the shims, leaving the two halves bearing the imprint of the figure. After the two halves were glued together with wet plaster, the hollow mold was filled with more wet plaster. When it was completely dry, the mold was chipped away to reveal the finished plaster figure.

Like other sculptors of the time,
Elisabet wanted the final figure
to be of marble because it was a
stone that would never crumble.
It would last forever,
while plaster cracked easily.

Since the finest marble was found in Europe, she sometimes took her plaster figures to Italy where marble was quarried. There the stonecutters made exact measurements of each figure and cut the marble to match. After bringing the marble figure back to Texas, Elisabet would add final details with special cutting tools, chisels, and hammers.

It took a long time to complete a statue. Elisabet was able to finish only the figure of Sam Houston for the Chicago fair. Texans were proud when the statue turned out to be one of the fair's most popular exhibits. They asked Miss Ney to make more statues of Texas heroes for the Austin capitol and for the nation's Capitol in Washington, D.C. Soon Elisabet had so many orders for her work that she built a large studio in Austin and made it her home.

In her studio, Elisabet spent the next fifteen years doing some of the best work of her life. Her last piece, a statue of Lady Macbeth, is now in the Smithsonian Institution in Washington, D.C. Other works are in museums and castles in Europe, at the University of Texas, in cemeteries, and in her Austin home.

Miss Ney's studio-home is now a museum filled with many of her sculptures and personal belongings. Streams of visitors go each year to see the works of the young woman who once said,

"I will be a sculptor."

THINKING
ABOUT IT

1. You are a reporter assigned to interview Elisabet Ney at her studio in Austin. What are the first questions you ask her?

2. Elisabet Ney had the courage to try new things and to be different from the people around her. What unusual things did Elisabet Ney do? Why were those things difficult to do during the time she lived?

3. Like Elisabet Ney, you are an artist asked to do a portrait of a famous Texan. Which Texan do you choose? What kind of a portrait will you do? Which materials will you use?

The Great Red River Raft

PETER ZACHARY COHEN

ILLUSTRATIONS BY JAMES WATLING

RED RIVER

RAFT

SHREVEPORT

MISSISSIPPI RIVER

TEXAS

About 400 years ago, or perhaps it was nearer 1,000—for no one really knows—the Red River was fat with spring rains. It had a bloody-muddy color from loosened red soil, and it was crowded with toppled trees caught in the flood and being carried from the plains and forests that are now called Texas, Oklahoma, Arkansas, and Louisiana, down toward the Gulf of Mexico.

Then—halfway across Louisiana—where the river made many curves a few trees got stuck at a river bend, then more trees became tangled against the few. After that, in the floods of each new year, still more floating trees locked their limbs together. They made a logjam, in some places as wide as the river and four times as tall as a man. It sank deep to the dark, muddy bottom yet stuck up in the warm, shady air.

Flood-by-flood that logjam grew longer, like a snake—adding new tangles to its tail every year, until it twisted up the Red River's channel across Louisiana, toward Texas, almost 200 miles. It forced the Red River to flow very slowly, and slow-moving water can't carry much mud. The mud stuck thickly in the tangled trees, forming dams, so the river had to flow sideways up streams, into lowlands, making long bayous, or swamps.

Meanwhile, on those soggy, mudded trunks of the logjam new trees and bushes began to grow so thickly that a deer or a bear or a man with a horse could walk on top, on narrow paths around some swamps amid the thick hum of bees and mosquitoes. The Caddo Indians and a few white settlers paddled the channels and stalked the trails there, finding many kinds of food and furs. But they had to be tough and smart and patient to travel that world very far without getting lost among the alligators.

Then came the steamboats! Glowing with fire, tossing smoke, churning the water behind them. They came hundreds of miles from New Orleans, St. Louis, Pittsburgh, and they aimed to go up the Red River toward Texas with supplies for new farms, towns, and forts. They waited for high water, then tried to work through the tangles. They charged up flooded bayous—and broke against hidden logs. Or got trapped in too-narrow passes, or just got lost for so long that the floods passed, the water drained away, and many boats mired forever amid that giant logjam men were calling the Great Red River Raft.

Oh, sure, there were *trails* to Texas, slow cart trails over steep hills into stagnant bogs, where men tossed in sleep through muggy nights while mosquitoes brought diseases with their stings and overworked animals died from the heat. So don't seek *your* fortune in Texas with only weak oxen to haul what you'd sell. You'd only go *broke* in Texas unless big steamboats got near there too. The steamboats *tried*—but most sank or were lost in the Great Red River Raft.

The Raft, *blast* the Raft, get rid of the Raft! Twice Army engineers slogged and rowed around it, and wrote that a million dollars spent could not remove it. That Raft was there to stay.

Then in the spring of 1833 upstream came Henry Shreve on a clumsy, broad, two-bottomed boat that he'd named the *Archimedes*. It looked like a crouching water bug and was twice as long as some houses. He stood out plainly on its open decks, a stout man with a lionlike head and a roaring idea: that *he* would get steamboats to Texas.

"How?" people asked. "Can't you see that Raft? There's two hundred miles of those stone-heavy logs all bound up in mud and woven together by the roots of new-grown trees. But *you'll* pull it apart to let us through and do it all in a year or two—? Oh, yes, you say. Oh, *sure* you will." Some laughed, some scowled, some shook their heads. Well—even today it's hard to believe there was such a man as Henry Shreve.

Where had he come from, this Henry Shreve, to challenge that giant jam? He'd grown up on rivers further north when boats had no engines at all. He'd learned how to lead different crews of rough men steering cargoes downstream, hauling loads upstream all by hand, more than 1,000 miles each way. Those small loads were heavy, and each trip took months, which made the goods costly for buying or selling. So the people who waited could afford less and less. Things *had* to move faster than that.

Then after 1807, news came to those inland valleys of exciting *steam*boats invented in New York's harbors! Soon men were steaming up the Mississippi, toward the Ohio—but the smooth river currents were somehow too strong, and the shifting shallow sandbars would not let them by.

Their boats struggled, then wore out, or ran aground. And Henry Shreve watched them, till he clearly saw why. Those boats were invented on sea coasts, he thought. Their engines and cargoes were deep down inside to keep the boats steady in huge ocean waves. "But these rivers," he said, "are not oceans. Why not build a boat that is *different?*"

So Henry Shreve went home to Brownsville, Pennsylvania, and began inventing blunt-bottomed, shallow-floating boats, and for them he tried different kinds of engines that he made work on the deck, *not* down in a hull. The engines were many times lighter, and burned half as much fuel, which left room on deck for some cargo besides. So then he built a tall upper story for people. "That'll make a boat tip," men said, and refused to invest. "No it won't," said Shreve, and refused to quit even when one of his early boats blew up.

It threw Shreve in the water and killed thirteen persons because a tiny weight had slipped on a safety valve. But Shreve rebuilt and kept on sailing. Once, he steamed from New Orleans to Louisville, up the Mississippi and Ohio, and returned south so fast that people thought he'd had to turn back part way. Well—even today it's hard to believe there was such a man as Henry Shreve, whose boats changed a haul of a hard four months into a jaunt of ten days.

That wasn't all to the good, of course, because soon hundreds of people were drowning each year as more and more new steamboats sailed those rivers and miles of hidden half-sunken driftlogs swayed up and down in the strong currents

spearing boats as they passed, like fish. And the Army warned it would need clear rivers to move soldiers in case of war. So thousands of dollars were offered for a plan to get rid of those snags.

For three years others *tried* to clear the channels with explosions and hand-levers and saws. They got nowhere—the money was running low— then the Army's chief paid attention to Shreve. He got the job, he started work by building an iron-coated *snagboat* that powered its paddles, its saws, and its chains by steam. And in 1831, two years from when he'd begun, along twelve-hundred river miles several thousand deadly spears were gone.

So now, in 1833, here he came up the Red River, again leading a crew of rough and daring men that he'd hired anywhere he could find them to help open a path to fortune for others with hard work that paid twenty dollars a month. And the gray soot fumed up from the iron chimneys, black crows flapped away through the trees, the snagboat's furnace fires crackled, its steam hissed and knocked through the pipes, its drive shafts thunked and rumbled, but those men rode silent and uncertain—

For there, straight ahead, yes they saw *it*, with the river clenched deep in *its* grip: rich with the smell of new flowers and old rot, alive with flashes of bright birds and mosquitoes, throbbing with hidden fish, and mink, and bear, and puma, mysterious with trailing vines and ghosts; huge and strong, and heavy, and jagged, patiently waited the Red River Raft.

Stoutly Henry Shreve stood on his snagboat, *Archimedes*, which was two of his broad-bottomed hulls held side-by-side, and eleven feet apart, by two levels of extra-strong beams. On top of each hull, beneath each furnace's roof, heated boilers were crowding steam through narrow pipes into larger cylinders and pushing each engine's sliding pistons back and forth, back and forth, thereby cranking the paddlewheels round.

And over the gap between the hulls were tall, powerful windlass reels that the steam could turn to

wind in, or out, long, strong, and heavy iron chains. And down between the front of the hulls was a solid wedge of timber and iron that aimed its sharp edge forward—this wedge was the snagboat's tusk.

Up on the deck Shreve stood and stared. Then he chose, and he pointed at one of the oldest logs in the Raft: "That one!" he shouted. "Full steam ahead!" Then the boilers roared and the cranking rods stroked. The paddlewheel blades threw back a foaming wake that spread and glittered in the springtime sun to beat on the shady shore, while under its stormy cloud of smoke sprouting from the two separate chimneys, the snagboat rammed its iron-capped tusk low and hard toward that ancient log.

That log had been helping to hold back floods for hundreds of years. It had never been struck at from below. It jerked up from the force of the ram, and perhaps from the force of surprise. The chains were shackled around it. Shreve's windlasses tore it loose and pulled it on board to the waiting saws that squealed when they tore at the old wet wood.

"Now *that* one!" Shreve ordered. His boat charged again—but that next log barely shifted—it bounced the snagboat back. "Again!" Shreve commanded. Again they charged. The log kicked like a wounded horse and still did not come loose. Then his men got in skiffs, and swarmed onto that timber fort like ants. They began sawing, and axing, and sweating. Then they called for the snagboat again.

"Again!" shouted Shreve. Again they rammed. The boat struck the log with a *Crack!* They jimmied it free, hauled it aboard, and the saws chewed it up for fuel, while the men on the Raft tried to rest in hot exhaustion. But suddenly things began to shake, to tremble, and gurgle, and slide—

"What's this?" men screamed, and leaped for the skiffs. An earthquake! some thought—or was it, instead, the first angry growl of the ancient ghosts of the Raft? "You brought us here," some shouted at Shreve. "Now get us away and fast!"

But Shreve yelled, "We're staying!" as the surge of water poured through the weakened place in the Raft, leaving two more logs floating free. "Can't you see?" shouted Shreve. "The river's helping. We've let the current move faster, so it loosened those logs. This is how I hoped we could win!"

Well—they tried again, and the more wood they untangled the stronger the river could flow, pushing logs loose on its own. That made it more risky, those slipping trees, but the work went faster along, so that even before summer had arrived Shreve and his men had rammed eighty miles. They had yanked open *nearly half of the Raft!*

But the Red River began drying up; the snagboat had to flee. Shreve couldn't return till more floods, with more logs, had re-jammed much of what he'd opened. Then people complained that the work went too slow, it cost too much, could never be done. And men who hadn't broken bones, or else been taken ill, grew sick of stenches stirred

from rotting vegetation, of the painful bites from bees swarming up from broken logs, of the chafe from wetted clothing that never seemed to dry, of cringing from the lightning striking fire near their boats—for a hundred varied reasons men grew weary till they quit, never to return.

So Shreve, who would rather captain a boat, had to write letters begging the Government for more money so he could keep trying. He had to keep doctoring crews, and finding more men, had to leave things unfinished when the river grew dry, then clear out over and over what more floods had put back. It was useless, hopeless—madness. Yet again and again, from season to season, by fits, stops, and starts, he kept at it.

Till in the spring of 1838—five years from when he'd begun, while muskrats swam off in a squeaky panic that scattered their shedding fur, Shreve's snagboat lunged through the last long limb into wide clear water upstream. Three loaded steamboats were already close behind him. The Red River Raft—it was no more. The trade to Texas was on!

It wasn't all for the best, of course, for the unclogged river went much faster than before, gouging its bed, draining the land, and causing floods afar downstream, while the men and beasts who'd lived with the Raft saw their dried swamps plowed into cotton fields, their forests cleared to make way for towns. Surrounded by newcomers at every turn, they found few places left to hunt, or even to hide, as the steamboats kept churning along, bringing cotton gins and grand pianos and the latest news and medicines.

And on a dry bluff above the Red River,
where some snagboat supplies had once been stored,
one new town grew with the name of Shreveport,
Louisiana. While Henry Shreve—he settled with
his family at St. Louis. There he began talking of
steamboats running on land, for against the sky he
began to see the smoke of new engines coming fast
on iron rails. The railroads grew, yet for many
years along all the rivers that he had opened for
safer, better travel, people at the landings saw the
tall boats come and leave, and rode them as far as
Montana—thanks to Henry Shreve.

Henry Miller Shreve
(October 21, 1785–March 6, 1851)

Henry Shreve was a breaker of barriers. In
1788, at the age of three, he rode in his family's wagon
on a rough trip over the Allegheny Mountains. His
father, Colonel Israel Shreve, had broken the teachings
of their Quaker religion by taking up weapons in war
(the American Revolution) and refusing to be sorry. So
the family had to leave their New Jersey community
and move to western Pennsylvania. As he grew up
there, Henry broke away from farming to work on
boats floating down those big western rivers—the
Monongahela, the Ohio, and the Mississippi.

When he was twenty-two he broke a tradition of the fur trade. It was the custom for Western fur traders to steer loads of hides downstream from St. Louis to New Orleans; from there sailing ships would carry them around the tip of Florida to market in Philadelphia. It was a long roundabout journey. So Henry Shreve built his own river keelboat, hired a crew, and began hauling furs by hand *up*stream on the Ohio to Pittsburgh, where he sent them on by wagon to Philadelphia. (There were no motors in those days.) He made money because his route was so much shorter than the old route.

Yet hauling boats upstream by hand was slow and hard work. As soon as Shreve heard of the invention of the steamboat, he began inventing steam-powered boats of his own. During the War of 1812 he used a steamboat he'd helped build to break through enemy barriers in heavy fogs. He aided other Americans defending New Orleans from capture by the British.

And right after peace came, Shreve found he had to break a *legal* barrier in New Orleans. Robert Fulton (who'd built the first successful steamboat in America) had obtained a charter which said that now only his steamboats could operate on the lower Mississippi, in and out of the New Orleans port. Shreve captained a boat into New Orleans anyway. He risked arrest and risked having his boat taken away. But with the help of a good lawyer and public opinion (Shreve had gained many friends while fighting the British), he made it too expensive and difficult for Fulton to keep him, and other boatmen, from using the river. Later the Supreme Court ruled that Fulton's charter had been unconstitutional.

By then Shreve was taking the lead in changing ideas about the way boats should be built. He helped design new shapes for boats and new ways of using machinery, so that steamboats could dependably force their way upstream against the strong currents and over the shallow sandbars of the inland rivers. He designed the *snagboats* that made it possible to remove all the dangerous old trees that had become sunken in the channels. Without Henry Shreve's different boats, which made thousands of miles of rivers easier, safer, faster, and cheaper for traveling, the young United States would have had a much harder time making use of—and holding onto—its vast inland empire.

Yet Shreve wasn't always successful. When he retired (after battling the Great Raft) he had enough money to buy a farm and invest in warehouses, but he had never been paid for all the uses that had been made of the snagboat design he'd patented. He tried for ten years to get the money but died before any payment ever came. Nor was all of his life happy. Medical science was not as advanced then as now. One by one he saw his first wife, three of his four children, and most of his grandchildren die. And today—in spite of his accomplishments and the fact that a town was named for him—hardly anyone knows his name.

PULLING IT ALL TOGETHER

1. Things sure changed after that Raft was cleared away! Are you glad Henry Shreve succeeded in clearing it? Why or why not?

2. The people who settled in Texas in the 1800s helped make the state what it is today. Why was it so important to these settlers that the Red River be cleared of the giant logjam?

3. You can jump into any of the selections in this book. You can help Little Gopher paint the colors of the setting sun, or help make tamales, or travel with Elisabet Ney. It's up to you. Which selection will you visit? What will you do while you are there?

The stars at night are big and bright,
DEEP IN THE HEART OF TEXAS;
The prairie sky is wide and high,
DEEP IN THE HEART OF TEXAS.
The sage in bloom is like perfume,
DEEP IN THE HEART OF TEXAS;
Reminds me of the one I love,
DEEP IN THE HEART OF TEXAS.

The coyotes wail along the trail,
DEEP IN THE HEART OF TEXAS;
The rabbits rush around the brush,
DEEP IN THE HEART OF TEXAS.
The cowboys cry, "Ki yip pee yi,"
DEEP IN THE HEART OF TEXAS.
The dogies bawl, and bawl, and bawl,
DEEP IN THE HEART OF TEXAS.

BOOKS TO ENJOY

Pecos Bill Rides a Tornado
by Wyatt Blassingame

When a tornado picks up Pecos Bill's house, the trees nearby, and even the Pecos River, Pecos Bill sets out to teach that pesky tornado a lesson.

Barbara Jordan: Keeping Faith
by Linda Jacobs

Barbara Jordan always meant to do something special with her life. She certainly succeeded! Follow Jordan's career from a law office in her parents' kitchen in Houston, Texas, to Congress in Washington, D.C.

The ABC's of Texas Wildflowers
by Glenna Gardiner Grimmer

This book shares interesting facts and detailed illustrations of twenty-six Texas wildflowers.

Spanish Pioneers of the Southwest
by Joan Anderson
Photographs by George Ancona

Before the Pilgrims arrived at Plymouth, Spanish settlers were living in what is now the southwestern part of the United States. With help from each family member, they managed to thrive in their new home.

Ganzy Remembers
by Mary Grace Ketner

Great-grandmother Ganzy loves to tell stories about her youth in the Texas Hill Country. Her great-granddaughter loves to listen.

The Tiguas
by Stan Steiner

Most people thought that a tribe of Texas Indians called the Tiguas was gone forever. But they have been living secretly near El Paso for hundreds of years. Read this book to find out how the tribe has survived.

The Day the Circus Came to Lone Tree
Written and illustrated by Glen Rounds

The circus was finally coming to Lone Tree. The townspeople could hardly control their excitement. They got even more excitement than they expected!

Oil and Gas: From Fossils to Fuels
by Hershell and Joan Lowery Nixon

Follow the story of oil and gas from their origins before the dinosaurs roamed the earth to their use in our cars, our homes, and even in wigs and toothbrushes.

LITERARY TERMS

Character

A **character** is a person, an animal, or even an object with human traits that has a part in a story. Some characters are round characters; that means you learn a lot about them. Others are flat characters; they don't change much. Their main purpose is to move readers through a story. Think about Shirley and Claude in *You Bet Your Britches, Claude*. Are they round characters or flat characters?

Conflict

Characters have **conflicts,** or struggles, that are part of the plot of the story in which they appear. Characters can struggle against other characters, against things in nature, or against themselves. Little Gopher struggles against himself in *The Legend of the Indian Paintbrush* when he tries to paint colors as bright as the ones in his dream.

Essay

An **essay** is a composition about a subject the writer has chosen to describe, criticize, or try to figure out. Often an essay expresses personal feelings. Most essays are rather short. Marisa Perales's essay in this book, "Visiting Huelo y Huela," is both short and personal.

Genre

A **genre** is a kind or type of literature that shares common characteristics. For example, tall tale is one genre. Tall tales include exaggeration and humor. Here are some genres included in this anthology: legend, biography, essay, historical fiction, nonfiction.

Interview

An **interview** is a kind of meeting in which one person (the interviewer) asks another person questions to get information. The interviewer might use the information to write an article or do a television or radio show. One of the hardest parts of doing an interview is to ask the right questions so that the information is accurate, easy to understand, and interesting. Are the questions from *An Interview with the Chinese Texans* good ones? Is the information interesting and understandable?

Legend

Many groups of people have traditional stories, often based on things that really happened, that they pass along from parents to children to grandchildren and so on through the generations. These traditional stories are called **legends.** *The Legend of the Indian Paintbrush* is an American Indian legend retold by Tomie dePaola.

GLOSSARY

Vocabulary from your selections

a·blaze (ə blāz′), **1** on fire; blazing: *The forest was set ablaze by lightning.* **2** shining brightly. *adjective.*

a·bun·dance (ə bun′dəns), great plenty; quantity that is more than enough. *noun.*

a·cad·e·my (ə kad′ə mē), **1** a private high school. **2** a school where some special subject can be studied. *noun, plural* **a·cad·e·mies.**

ad·mis·sion (ad mish′ən), **1** an allowing to enter: *His admission into the hospital was delayed for lack of beds.* **2** the price paid for the right to enter. **3** an admitting to be true; confession. *noun.*

an·ces·tor (an′ses′tər), a person from whom one is directly descended. Your grandfathers, your grandmothers, and so on back, are your ancestors. *noun.*

ap·point (ə point′), to name for an office or position; choose. *verb.*

a·re·na (ə rē′nə), **1** a space or building in which certain contests or sports are held. **2** a building in which indoor sports are played. *noun.*

arena (definition 1)

a·ro·ma (ə rō′mə), a fragrance; spicy odor. *noun.*

blunt (blunt), **1** without a sharp edge or point; dull: *a blunt knife.* **2** to make less sharp; make less keen. **3** saying what one thinks very frankly, without trying to be polite; outspoken. **1,3** *adjective,* **2** *verb.*

boil·er (boi′lər), a tank for making steam to heat buildings or drive engines. *noun.*

break (brāk), **1** to come apart or make come apart; smash. **2** to train to obey; tame: *to break a colt. verb,* **breaks, broke, bro·ken, break·ing.**

britch·es (brich′iz), pants; trousers. *noun plural.*

bro·ken (brō′kən), **1** separated into parts by a break; in pieces: *a broken cup.* **2** not in working condition; damaged: *a broken watch. adjective.*

buck·skin (buk′skin′), a strong, soft leather, yellowish or grayish in color, made from the skins of deer or sheep. *noun.*

bun·dle (bun′dl), **1** a number of things tied or wrapped together: *a bundle of old newspapers.* **2** a parcel; package. **3** to tie or wrap together; make into a bundle. **1,2** *noun,* **3** *verb,* **bun·dled, bun·dling.**

can·yon (kan′yən), a narrow valley with high, steep sides, usually with a stream at the bottom. *noun.*

a hat	i it	oi oil	ch child	ə stands for:
ā age	ī ice	ou out	ng long	a in about
ä far	o hot	u cup	sh she	e in taken
e let	ō open	ù put	th thin	i in pencil
ē equal	ô order	ü rule	ŦH then	o in lemon
ėr term			zh measure	u in circus

canyon—The Grand **Canyon**

ca·pa·ble (kā′pə bəl), able; having fitness, power, or ability. *adjective.*

Cap·i·tol (kap′ə təl), **1** the building at Washington, D.C., in which Congress meets. **2** Also, **capitol.** the building in which a state legislature meets. *noun.*

car·go (kär′gō), the load of goods carried by a ship or plane. *noun, plural* **car·goes** or **car·gos.**

chan·nel (chan′l), **1** the deeper part of a waterway: *There is shallow water on both sides of the channel in this river.* **2** the bed of a stream or river: *Rivers cut their own channels to the sea.* **3** a body of water joining two larger bodies of water. **4** a television station. *noun.*

chat·ty (chat′ē), fond of friendly, familiar talk. *adjective,* **chat·ti·er, chat·ti·est.**

churn (chėrn), **1** a container or machine in which butter is made from cream by beating and shaking. **2** to beat and shake cream in a churn. **3** to move as if beaten and shaken: *The water churns in the rapids.* **1** *noun,* **2,3** *verb.*

ci·ca·da (sə kā′də), a large insect with two pairs of thin, transparent wings. The male makes a shrill sound in hot, dry weather. Cicadas are commonly called locusts. *noun, plural* **ci·ca·das.**

creek (krēk *or* krik), a small stream. *noun.*

cro·chet (krō shā′), to make sweaters, lace, and other things by looping thread or yarn into links with a single hooked needle. *verb,* **cro·chets** (krō shāz′), **cro·cheted** (krō shād′), **cro·chet·ing** (krō shā′ing).

crys·tal (kris′tl), **1** a clear, transparent mineral that looks like ice. It is a kind of quartz. **2** clear and transparent like crystal: *crystal water.* **3** one of the regularly shaped pieces with angles and flat surfaces into which many substances solidify. **1,3** *noun,* **2** *adjective.*

dep·u·ty (dep′yə tē), a person appointed to do the work or take the place of another: *The sheriff appointed deputies to help him enforce the law. noun, plural* **dep·u·ties.**

de·sign (di zīn′), **1** a drawing, plan, or sketch made to serve as a pattern from which to work. **2** the arrangement of details, form, and color in painting, weaving, or building. **3** to make a first sketch of; plan out; arrange the form and color of. **1,2** *noun,* **3** *verb.*

drift (drift), **1** to carry or be carried along by currents of air or water: *A raft drifts if it is not steered.* **2** to go along without knowing or caring where one is going. **3** to heap or be heaped up by the wind. **4** snow or sand heaped up by the wind. 1-3 *verb,* 4 *noun.*

ef·fort (ef′ərt), **1** the use of energy and strength to do something; trying hard. **2** a hard try; strong attempt. *noun.*

ex·ist·ence (eg zis′təns), **1** the state or condition of being. **2** a being real: *Most people do not now believe in the existence of ghosts.* **3** life: *Drivers of racing cars lead a dangerous existence. noun.*

for·ma·tion (fôr mā′shən), **1** the forming, making, or shaping of something: *Heat causes the formation of steam from water.* **2** the way in which something is arranged; arrangement; order. **3** a thing formed: *Clouds are formations of tiny drops of water in the sky. noun.*

freeze (frēz), **1** to harden by cold; turn into a solid. **2** to make or become very cold. **3** to kill or injure by frost; be killed or injured by frost. **4** to cover or become covered with ice; clog with ice: *The pipes froze.* **5** to fix or become fixed to something by freezing: *His fingers froze to the tray of ice cubes.* **6** a freezing or a being frozen: *An early freeze damaged many gardens.* **7** to become motionless. 1-5,7 *verb,* **freez·es, froze, fro·zen, freez·ing;** 6 *noun.*

fu·ner·al (fyü′nər əl), the ceremonies held at the burial of a dead person. A funeral usually includes a religious service and taking the body to the place where it is buried or burned. *noun.*

ge·ol·o·gist (jē ol′ə jist), a person who is an expert in geology. *noun.*

ge·ol·o·gy (jē ol′ə jē), the science that deals with the composition and history of the earth, the moon, and similar heavenly bodies. The study of rocks is an important part of geology. *noun.*

gran·ite (gran′it), a very hard gray or pink rock, much used for buildings and monuments. Granite is made of crystals of several different minerals and is formed when lava cools slowly underground. *noun.*

granite—a chunk of **granite**

heir·loom (er′lüm′ *or* ar′lüm′), a possession handed down from generation to generation. *noun.*

his·tor·y (his′tər ē), a story or record of important past events that happened to a person or nation: *the history of the United States. noun, plural* **his·tor·ies.**

hull (hul), **1** the body or frame of a ship. **2** the outer covering of a seed. **3** the small leaves around the stem of a strawberry and certain other fruits. **4** to remove the hull or hulls from: *to hull berries.* 1-3 *noun,* 4 *verb.*

in·spi·ra·tion (in/spə rā/shən), **1** the influence of thought and strong feelings on actions, especially on good actions: *Some people get inspiration from nature.* **2** any influence that arouses effort or activity. **3** a sudden, brilliant idea. *noun.*

knead (nēd), **1** to press or mix together dough or clay into a soft mass. Kneading may be done with the hands or by machine. **2** to press and squeeze with the hands; massage. *verb.*

lard (lärd), the fat of pigs or hogs, melted down for use in cooking. *noun.*

le·gal (lē/gəl), **1** of law: *legal knowledge.* **2** of lawyers: *legal advice.* **3** according to law; lawful. *adjective.*

log·jam (lôg/jam/, log/jam/), **1** a blocking of the downstream movement of logs, causing a jumbled overcrowding of the timber in the river. **2** a deadlock or standstill. *noun.*

min·now (min/ō), **1** a very small freshwater fish. **2** any fish when it is very small. *noun.*

					ə stands for:
a hat	i it	oi oil	ch child		
ā age	ī ice	ou out	ng long		a in about
ä far	o hot	u cup	sh she		e in taken
e let	ō open	u̇ put	th thin		i in pencil
ē equal	ô order	ü rule	ᴛʜ then		o in lemon
ėr term			zh measure		u in circus

mod·el (mod/l), **1** a small copy of something: *A globe is a model of the earth.* **2** a figure in clay or wax that is to be copied in marble, bronze, or other material. **3** to make, shape, or fashion; design or plan. **4** a person who poses for artists and photographers. 1,2,4 *noun,* 3 *verb.*

mo·ral (môr/əl), **1** good in character or conduct; virtuous according to civilized standards of right and wrong; right; just: *a moral person.* **2** having to do with character or with the difference between right and wrong. **3** the lesson, inner meaning, or teaching of a fable, a story, or an event. 1,2 *adjective,* 3 *noun.*

na·tion·al (nash/ə nəl), of a nation; belonging to a whole nation: *national laws.* *adjective.*

no·to·ri·ous (nō tôr/ē əs), well-known or commonly known, especially because of something bad. *adjective.*

nui·sance (nü/sns or nyü/sns), a thing or person that annoys, troubles, offends, or is disagreeable. *noun.*

pas·try (pā/strē), **1** pies, tarts, or other baked food made with dough rich in butter or other shortening. **2** the dough for such food. *noun, plural* **pas·tries.**

peck (pek), **1** to strike at and pick up with the beak: *The hen pecked corn.* **2** a stroke made with the beak: *The canary gave me a peck.* **3** to make by striking with the beak. **4** a hole or mark made by pecking. **5** to make a pecking motion. **6** a quick kiss usually on the cheek. 1,3,5 *verb*, 2,4,6 *noun*.

per·fect (pėr′fikt *for 1,3-5, and 7;* pər fekt′ *for 2 and 6*), **1** having no faults; not spoiled at any point: *a perfect life.* **2** to remove all faults from; make perfect; add the finishing touches to: *to perfect an invention.* **3** completely skilled; expert. **4** having all its parts there; complete. **5** exact: *a perfect circle.* **6** to carry through; complete. **7** entire; complete: *She was a perfect stranger to us.* 1,3-5,7 *adjective*, 2,6 *verb*.

plain (plān), **1** clear; easy to understand; easily seen or heard: *The meaning is plain.* **2** clearly; in a plain manner. **3** without ornament or decoration; simple. **4** all of one color. **5** not rich or highly seasoned. **6** common; ordinary; simple in manner. **7** not pretty or handsome; homely: *a plain face.* **8** a flat stretch of land. 1,3-7 *adjective*, 2 *adverb*, 8 *noun*.

plan·ta·tion (plan tā′shən), a large farm or estate on which cotton, tobacco, sugar cane, or rubber trees are grown. The work on a plantation is done by laborers who live there. *noun*.

ram (ram), **1** a male sheep. **2** to butt against; strike head-on; strike violently. **3** to push hard; drive down or in by heavy blows. 1 *noun*, 2,3 *verb*, **rams, rammed, ram·ming.**

rare (rer *or* rar), **1** seldom seen, found, or happening: *Snow is rare in Florida.* **2** unusually good: *Edison had rare powers as an inventor.* **3** thin; not dense: *The higher we go above the earth, the rarer the air is.* *adjective*, **rar·er, rar·est.**

rare (definition 1)—This picture shows both sides of a **rare** Jewish coin that is almost 1900 years old.

re·ceipt (ri sēt′), **1** a written statement that money, a package, or a letter has been received. **2** to write on a bill or invoice that something has been received or paid for. **3 receipts,** the money received: *Our expenses were less than our receipts.* **4** a receiving. 1,3,4 *noun*, 2 *verb*.

re·cep·tion (ri sep′shən), **1** an act or manner of receiving: *She got a warm reception from her friend.* **2** a party or entertainment to welcome people. **3** the quality of the sound in a radio or sound and picture in a television set. *noun*.

re·verse (ri vėrs′), **1** the opposite or contrary. **2** turned backward; opposite or contrary in position or direction. **3** the back. **4** to turn the other way; turn inside out; turn upside down. 1,3 *noun*, 2 *adjective*, 4 *verb*, **re·vers·es, re·versed, re·vers·ing.**

sad·dle·bag (sad′l bag′), one of a pair of bags laid over an animal's back behind the saddle, or over the rear fender of a bicycle or motorcycle. *noun.*

sculp·tor (skulp′tər), a person who carves or models figures. *noun.*

sha·man (shä′mən, shā′mən, *or* sham′ən), **1** man in American Indian tribes who was believed to have close contact with the spirit world, and who was skilled in curing diseases; medicine man. **2** a similar man in certain other societies. *noun.*

snag (snag), **1** a tree or branch held fast in a river or lake. **2** any sharp or rough projecting point, such as the broken end of a branch. **3** to catch on a snag. **4** a hidden or unexpected obstacle. 1,2,4 *noun,* 3 *verb,* **snags, snagged, snag·ging.**

splin·ter (splin′tər), **1** a thin, sharp piece of wood, bone, glass, or the like. **2** to split or break into thin, sharp pieces. 1 *noun,* 2 *verb.*

spoil (spoil), **1** to damage or injure something so as to make it unfit or useless; ruin; destroy: *The rain spoiled the picnic.* **2** to be damaged; become bad or unfit for use. **3** to injure the character or disposition of. 1-3 *verb,* **spoils, spoiled** or **spoilt, spoil·ing.**

steer[1] (stir), **1** to guide the course of: *to steer a car.* **2** to be guided. **3** to direct one's way or course. *verb.*

steer[2] (stir), a young male of cattle raised for beef, usually two to four years old. *noun.*

sun·set (sun′set′), the last appearance of the sun at the end of day. *noun.*

a hat	i it	oi oil	ch child	ə stands for:
ā age	ī ice	ou out	ng long	a in about
ä far	o hot	u cup	sh she	e in taken
e let	ō open	u̇ put	th thin	i in pencil
ē equal	ô order	ü rule	ᵀH then	o in lemon
ėr term			zh measure	u in circus

tex·ture (teks′chər), the feel that cloth or other things have because of their structure. *noun.*

un·in·hab·it·ed (un′in hab′ə tid), not lived in; without inhabitants: *an uninhabited wilderness. adjective.*

vat (vat), a tank; large container for liquids: *a vat of dye. noun.*

veg·e·ta·tion (vej′ə tā′shən), plant life; growing plants. *noun.*

vi·sion (vizh′ən), **1** the power of seeing; sense of sight: *I have to wear glasses because my vision is poor.* **2** something that is seen. **3** the power of seeing with the imagination or by clear thinking, especially seeing what the future may bring. **4** something seen with the imagination, in a dream, or in one's thoughts. *noun.*

wedge (wej), **1** a piece of wood or metal thick at one end and tapering to a thin edge at the other. A wedge is driven in between objects to be separated or into anything to be split. **2** something shaped like a wedge or used like a wedge: *a wedge of pie.* **3** to split or separate with a wedge. **4** to fasten or tighten with a wedge. 1,2 *noun,* 3,4 *verb,* **wedg·es, wedged, wedg·ing.**

Acknowledgments

Text

Page 6: "The Texas Cowboy." Glendive, MT: *Glendive Independent,* March 31, 1988.

Page 8: *The Legend of the Indian Paintbrush* retold and illustrated by Tomie dePaola. Copyright © 1988 by Tomie dePaola. Reprinted by permission of G. P. Putnam's Sons.

Page 28: *Bill Pickett: First Black Rodeo Star.* Text copyright © 1977 by Sibyl Hancock. Reprinted by permission of Harcourt Brace Jovanovich, Inc.

Page 42: from *Mother Goose on the Rio Grande* by Frances Alexander, pp. 44–45. Copyright © 1988, 1977 by Passport Books, a division of NTC Publishing Group. Reprinted by permission.

Page 44: "Christmas Tamales" by Ray Gonzales. Copyright © by Ray Gonzales, 1991.

Page 50: *The Best Town in the World* by Byrd Baylor. Text copyright © 1982 Byrd Baylor. Illustrations copyright © 1983 Ronald Himler. Reprinted with the permission of Charles Scribner's Sons, an imprint of Macmillan Publishing Company.

Page 74: from *Who Are the Chinese Texans?* by Marian L. Martinello and William T. Field, Jr. Copyright © 1979 by The University of Texas. Reprinted by permission of The University of Texas, Institute of Texan Cultures at San Antonio.

Page 82: "Frost Flowers" from *Young Naturalist* by Ilo Hiller from *Texas Parks & Wildlife Magazine.* Copyright © 1983 by Texas A&M University Press. Reprinted by permission of Texas A&M University Press.

Page 88: "What It Means To Be Hispanic" by Marisa Perales, *Hispanic,* July 1989. Copyright © 1989 by the Hispanic Publishing Corporation. Reprinted by permission.

Page 94: "A Writer in Texas" by Joan Lowery Nixon. Copyright © by Joan Lowery Nixon, 1991.

Page 100: *You Bet Your Britches, Claude* by Joan Lowery Nixon, illustrated by Tracey Campbell Pearson. Copyright © 1989 by Joan Lowery Nixon for text. Copyright © 1989 by Tracey Campbell Pearson for illustrations. Used by permission of Viking Penguin, a division of Penguin Books USA, Inc.

Page 116: from *Apples on a Stick* collected and edited by Barbara Michels and Bettye White, illustrations by Jerry Pinkney. Copyright © 1983 by Barbara Michels & Bettye White, illustrations copyright © 1983 by Jerry Pinkney. Reprinted by permission of Coward-McCann, Inc.

Page 120: "Elisabet Ney: 1833–1907 Artist Against All Odds" from *Twenty Texans* by Betsy Warren, pp. 60–64. Copyright © 1985 Hendrick-Long Publishing Company. Reprinted by permission.

Page 128: *The Great Red River Raft* by Peter Zachary Cohen, illustrated by James Watling. Text copyright © 1984 by Peter Zachary Cohen. Illustrations copyright © 1984 James Watling. Reprinted by permission of the author and the illustrator.

Page 148: "Deep In The Heart Of Texas" by June Hershey & Don Swander. Copyright © 1941 Melody Lane Publications, Inc. Copyright renewed by Melody Lane Publications, Inc., 1740 Broadway, New York, NY 10019. International Copyright Secured. Made in U.S.A. All Rights Reserved.

Artists

Maria Stroster cover, 1–5, 94–99 (decorative art), 147, 150–152, 154
Regan Dunnick 6–7, 148–149
Tomie dePaola 8–27
Rex Parker 28–29 (border), 41, 75
Richard Leonard 28–40
Rose Johnson 42
Ann Morton Hubbard 44, 46–47
Jennie Oppenheimer 45–46, 49
Ronald Himler 50–69
Debbie Drechsler 74
Joel Nakamura 76, 81
Tracey Campbell Pearson 100–115
Jerry Pinkney 116–119
Betsy Warren 126
Charles Cashwell 128
James Watling 131–144

Photographs

Unless otherwise acknowledged, all photographs are the property of ScottForesman.

Pages 44 (inset), 47, 88, 90 (top), 91, 92 (both): Tim Street-Porter
Page 75: Jerry Valente
Page 77: Nik Kelsh/Kelsh Marr Studios
Page 78: Owen Franken/Stock Boston
Page 79: Patrick Tehan
Page 80: Elizabeth Crews/Stock Boston
Pages 82–87: Courtesy Texas Parks & Wildlife Department
Page 93: Courtesy Marisa Perales, Robstown High School
Page 94: Courtesy Texas Ranger Hall of Fame, Waco
Pages 94–99 map background photos: Map by Guenter Vollath. From *The Smithsonian Guide to Historic America: Texas and the Arkansas River Valley,* published by Stewart, Tabori & Chang. Reproduced by permission of the publisher.
Page 98: *East Side, Main Plaza, San Antonio, Texas 1849* by William G. M. Samuel, San Antonio Museum Association, Witte Memorial Museum.
Page 121: Texas State Library, Austin, Texas
Page 122: Jack Puryear Photography
Page 124: Courtesy of Elisabet Ney Museum, Austin, Texas
Page 125: Bob Daemmrich
Page 155: Jean-Francois Causse/Tony Stone Worldwide

Glossary

The contents of the glossary have been adapted from *Beginning Dictionary,* Copyright © 1988 Scott, Foresman and Company.